Praise for

The Mediator's Toolkit

All the most important conflicts we face today, from war and politics to workplace and domestic disputes, are sparked by the brain's responses to conflict. In the last few years, groundbreaking neurophysiological research has led to profound new understandings of how the brain works, and to immensely creative, powerful new ways of responding to conflict. Gerry O'Sullivan has written a wonderful, well-researched, fascinating and practical toolkit for mediators that offers fresh new insights into how we can help our brains discover the questions that can transform conflicts into opportunities for resolution, learning and improved relationships. It is a terrific read, and one you will relish and be grateful for.

— Kenneth Cloke, mediator and author of *The Dance of Opposites: Explorations in Mediation, Dialogue and Conflict Resolution Systems Design.*

An invaluable analysis, not merely of questions, but of a range of process interventions, to equip mediators in all sectors to deepen the effectiveness of their work with people in dispute. Mediators have to work in the moment, exercising their intuition in a flash as to what to do next and how. This book will help to develop the internal base from which such intuitive insights emerge.

— Tony Allen, Mediator and Senior Consultant to CEDR, London

As a mediator and trainer this is a must have book. It fills a gap in the literature that has long been ignored but goes to the heart of mediating conflicts. *The Mediator's Toolkit: Formulating and Asking Questions for Successful Outcomes* strikes the right balance between theory and practice making sure mediators know what to ask; why these questions are important; and the theoretical foundations of the cognitive shift the questions seek to initiate. O'Sullivan's examples and cases are reflective of a mediator's reality making the toolkit a valuable book to buy in hardcover and keep on the desk.

— Dr. Juan Diaz-Prinz, Mediator and Trainer in Conflict Management, Berlin, Germany

The Mediator's Toolkit is a rare thing indeed — a practical manual built on a solid foundation of knowledge and theory. Set out in an engaging, user friendly format, this book fills a crucial gap in mediation skills and practice — knowing WHY and HOW different questions work at various junctures in mediation, instead of just providing a list of interventions. Drawing on cutting edge research in psychology and neuroscience, this book gives both novice and experienced mediators new insight into their practice, and a concrete and easy to use model for improving this practice and developing their skills to a very high level. This book is essential reading for all students of conflict and mediation, and should have a place in the briefcase of every practising mediator, no matter how experienced.

— Sabine Walsh, President, Mediators' Institute of Ireland,
Course Director, MA Conflict Management, St. Angela's College Sligo

Questioning is often an unknown territory that O'Sullivan unravels. *The Mediator's Toolkit* is a most welcome, useful, and sophisticated addition to the mediation and conflict coaching field. It synthesizes and explains the tools that are most relevant to questions in a user friendly, while intelligent fashion, with a view to practice. It will be a reference book for the serious hands-on professional for years to come.

— Dr. Antje Herrberg, CEO, Mediateur; Adjunct Professor in Peace Mediation,
College of Europe; Former Member of the UN Standby Team for Mediation

During my 24 years of mediating, I have always felt there has been insufficient attention given to the role of effective use of questions as part of the mediator's toolkit. Indeed in my experience most mediator training and texts only pay cursory attention to this skill-set. *The Mediator's Toolkit* skillfully and clearly fills this gap. It provides mediators with a clear conceptual framework to structure their questioning, clearly sets out the theoretical and psychological underpinnings to these techniques and then in some detail gives practical examples of how these questions may be used in mediation. While clearly written with mediators in mind, it is an invaluable resources to all those looking to resolve conflict.

— James South, Mediator and Managing Director,
The Centre for Effective Dispute Resolution (CEDR), London

THE
Mediator's Toolkit
FORMULATING *and*
ASKING QUESTIONS
for Successful Outcomes

GERRY O'SULLIVAN

new society
PUBLISHERS

Cover design by Diane McIntosh.
Cover images (question marks): ©iStock:139378660; 149150786; 154137367; 177342698; 453903049; 473634274; 480113679; 495066924; 499632216; 540519136; 576715772; 700929440; 822694260; 8 27147872; 888184030

Images: © Simon Olley
Water background © adobestock_67829647; Beach background © MJ Jessen

First printing September 2018.   Printed in Canada

Any other inquiries can be directed by mail to:
New Society Publishers
P.O. Box 189, Gabriola Island, BC V0R 1X0, Canada
(250) 247-9737

LIBRARY AND ARCHIVES CANADA CATALOGUING IN PUBLICATION

O'Sullivan, Gerry, 1953-, author
        The mediator's toolkit : formulating and asking questions
for successful outcomes / Gerry O'Sullivan.

Includes bibliographical references and index.
Issued in print and electronic formats.
ISBN 978-0-86571-897-5 (softcover).--ISBN 978-1-55092-690-3
(PDF).--ISBN 978-1-77142-286-4 (EPUB)

        1. Mediation--Handbooks, manuals, etc. 2. Negotiation--Handbooks, manuals, etc. 3. Conflict management--Handbooks, manuals, etc. I. Title.

HM1126.O88 2018   303.6'9   C2018-902685-5
                                       C2018-902686-3

Funded by the Government of Canada   Financé par le gouvernement du Canada

New Society Publishers' mission is to publish books that contribute in fundamental ways to building an ecologically sustainable and just society, and to do so with the least possible impact on the environment, in a manner that models this vision.

To my wonderful sons Raymond and Carl

Contents

Acknowledgments

I HAVE TWO WONDERFUL SONS: Raymond, who keeps grammar books in the bathroom as he likes grammar so much and seems to consider the subject as light, entertaining reading, and Carl, who is qualified as a mediator. I discovered very early on that the skills of both of my sons were extremely valuable in supporting me in writing a book on mediation. At this stage, I bet they are both very relieved the project is over and they can return to their peaceful lives. The incisiveness and quality of their work provided immense and valuable support, and I thank them and appreciate that they were there when I needed them. Above all, I thank them for their extreme patience.

The patience of Raymond and Carl was finely matched by that of my graphic designer, Simon Olley. I know I sorely tested him in the last four and three-quarter years. I never thought it was possible for any one human being to change their mind so many times, but I did, and Simon met every one with politeness, gentleness and enormous patience. I am deeply appreciative of his very talented and astute mind.

During that first year when I was researching our physiological responses to conflict, I relied heavily on the expertise of Germaine Staunton, and also on Janice Tucker — thank you to both of them.

The plan for this book was to start and finish it in four months, but, oh dear, it is now four and three-quarter years! At the end of Year One, I sent the draft to mediator friends and colleagues, assuming that in a couple of weeks I would have made all their suggested amendments and my work would be finished. But my friend Cora Carrigg had different ideas and spent five hours telling me how the book needed serious restructuring! The kindest thing I could say to myself after Cora's forensic work was that I had developed a training manual but had not taken into account that I would not be there with the reader to deliver it. The worst I can admit to myself is that no publishing house would have touched this book in the form it was after that first year. I then spent more than three years working on it to whip it into shape, so thank you for your enormous help and feedback, Cora.

I would particularly like to thank those who so kindly gave me specialist help: David Walsh (NLP), Judy Rees (Clean Language), Janis Magnusson and Peter Greene (publishing) and Sabrina Spillane (IT support). Thank you for your generous spirits and your time.

To those who gave me feedback on particular sections of the book — Mary Lou O'Kennedy, Mary Rafferty, Ann Walsh, Ray Flaherty, Paul Pierse, Derek Windram, Siun Kearney, Helen Harnett and Vera Hogan — I would like to extend to you all warm and sincere thanks for taking this time from your own worlds to do so.

Thank you to those I have trained to become mediators as I have learned so much from you over the years and thank you for your feedback on the S Questions Model.

And thank you to Ken Cloke for believing in me from the start, and for "giving the dumb priest the parish"!

I would also like to extend my appreciation to the staff of New Society Publishers.

Glossary

Affect labeling: Describing feelings with words.

Amygdala: Our threat detector, and it calculates whether a stimulus is to be feared and avoided, or whether something is a reward and can be approached.

Approach-reward reflex: Humans are hardwired to minimize or avoid pain and maximize reward. If people sense that there is a reward, they will unconsciously and automatically experience an approach-reward reflex.

Attitude: The way a person expresses or applies their beliefs and values.

Avoid-threat reflex: Humans are hard-wired to minimize or avoid pain and maximize reward. If people sense a threat, they will unconsciously and automatically experience an avoid-threat reflex. If a threat is perceived, the sympathetic nervous system is stimulated and prepares to meet that stressful situation, including triggering a fight or flight response, as necessary.

Belief: An internal feeling that something is true, even though it may be unproven or irrational.

Caucus: A separate private meeting that is held with a party during a joint meeting.

Clean Language: The Clean Language questioning technique is a method used for seeking information while ensuring that a mediator's own perceptions, assumptions or bias do not taint the questions posed. It consists of a set of simple questions, asked in a specific way, using the client's own words and symbols.

Cognition: Any knowledge, opinion or belief that is held by a person regarding their sense of self or identity, or their behavior or environment.

Cognitive elements: The six cognitive elements are: knowledge; opinions and thinking; beliefs, values and attitudes; behavior; sense of self or identity; and environment (the physical, social or psychological world in which a person lives).

Cognitive dissonance: The psychological conflict that results when one cognitive element is incongruent with another cognitive element, simultaneously.

Cognitive consonance: When cognitive elements are congruent with each other.

Conflict trigger: An event that results in a sudden and disproportionate emotional reaction in a person. This emotional reaction indicates that something that is of fundamental value to the person is perceived to be, or is, under threat.

Future Focus question: A question used to generate connections with a possible future perspective. These questions paint a hypothetical, conditional or consequential picture on which parties in conflict can reflect. Future-focus questions change the parties' states of mind and bring them to a place where they can look at their conflict differently, from outside their current paradigm.

Journey of Inference: The inner journey a person makes from the time they experience something to the decisions they make based on that experience. This journey encompasses the information they selected during the experience; the interpretations they made about that information; the assumptions they made; and the conclusions they then reached, which, in turn, informed any decisions or actions they took.

Metaphor: A figure of speech in which a word or phrase is applied to an object or action to which it is not literally applicable, for example, "It is raining cats and dogs."

Neuro-linguistic Programming (NLP): NLP encompasses the three most influential components involved in producing human experience: neurology, language and programming. The neurological system regulates how bodies function, language determines how people interact and communicate with other people, and programming determines what kinds of models of the world they create. NLP describes the fundamental dynamics between mind (neuro) and language (linguistic), and how their interplay affects body and behavior (programming).

Paradigm: A person's model for interpreting and understanding their world, their role in it and how they understand the roles of others. In NLP terms this is called their world map.

Paradigm shift: When a person changes their thinking, perspective and understanding about something.

PEP interaction: The interaction between the people involved in a conflict, the environment or context in which the conflict takes place and the problem presenting.

Position: The stance a party takes in a conflict. This is the place from where they rationalize their situation, and then act and react. When a party is feeling threatened, the "position" they take will be their way of protecting their vulnerability.

Unconscious: Any thought or emotion that happens outside everyday awareness.

Underlying interest: The deep-down need or fear that informs and drives the stance or "position" a party adopts in a conflict.

Values: A measure of the worth or importance people attach to something.

Introduction

The Purpose of This Book

THIS BOOK INTRODUCES THE S QUESTIONS MODEL, which focuses on the development and asking of questions for clarifying existing information, gathering new information and creating new insight in parties.

For parties in mediation to reach an effective and sustainable agreement, they need to experience a change in their thinking about their conflict. Such a paradigm shift happens when a person looks at a situation in a different way. This shift in a party's thinking and approach is achieved when they gain new information and insight that leads them to look at their conflict from a different perspective.

The S Questions Model is designed to house a toolkit of questions that can be asked during a mediation process. This book demonstrates the theory behind the question types, their purpose, how they work, when they are used and how they are built and applied to mediation. The S Questions Model is an easily accessible reference tool for a mediator, both before and during a mediation process.

Book Content

The book is split into four sections:

Section 1: The S Questions Model — Theory
Section 2: Practical Application of the S Questions Model
Section 3: Practical Application of S1, S2 and S3 Questions
Section 4: Practical Application of S4 Questions

While this is primarily a book that demonstrates the S Questions Model for use in mediation, the learning from this book is broader than the development and asking of questions. Theories from neuroscience and psychology are explored as a means of solidly embedding the development of the S Questions Model in a sound theoretical context.

For example, Chapter 2: How We Process and Communicate Information describes how our brain processes only 40 bits of information per second out of the 11 million bits available to us. This deficit of information highlights the importance of asking strategic, incisive questions to bring new information into a mediation process so that parties gain new insight and achieve a paradigm shift in their thinking. This chapter builds the case to prove that we live within a reality that has serious information deficit.

Chapter 3: Working with the Brain in Mediation provides a description of the inner physiological state of parties in conflict when they are feeling under threat. The chapter illustrates how to manage this so that parties feel less threatened, can think cognitively and can get to the core of their conflict. It is only by identifying the core of the conflict that appropriate and sustainable solutions can be found and agreed upon.

Knowing the theoretical context on which the S Questions Model was built will enhance the reader's understanding of the model, and its applicability to mediation.

Terminology

"Pre-mediation"

This book is based on the premise that a mediation process starts when the parties agree with the mediator to engage in a mediation process, even though the formal signing of the Agreement to Mediate contract may not happen until the first separate private meeting; therefore, the term *pre-mediation* is not used in this book.

"Separate Meeting" or "Separate Private Meeting"

These terms are used in this book for both the initial separate private meetings that take place before the first joint meeting and for the separate private meetings that take place during a joint meeting. The separate private meeting that takes place during the joint meetings is also commonly known as a "caucus meeting."

"Joint Meeting" or "Plenary Meeting"

The term "joint meeting," rather than "plenary meeting," is used throughout the book.

Sequences of Questions

The Use of Academic Terminology

Some of the terminology used in this book is academic and will need to be substituted with simpler language when posing questions to parties in real-life mediation.

The questions introduced in this book are templates that demonstrate the possible questions that could be asked under a variety of circumstances. While a mediator may introduce a specific topic with a chosen question, subsequent questions will need to be informed by the party's response to the initial question.

Listening effectively to a party is what will suggest a mediator's next question, rather than adhering to a question template, which merely serves as a guide for the mediator. In conclusion, questions should not be rigidly based on a script or a template from this book.

Section I

The S Questions Model — Theory

Introduction and Purpose of the S Questions Model

The S Questions Model

THE S QUESTIONS MODEL was developed to incorporate the wide range of questions that can be asked during a mediation process into one clear and accessible image. This image can be utilized by a mediator to identify the most appropriate question to ask in any given circumstance. The S Questions Model forms the context in which the learning from the theory in Section 1 of this book is applied. Sections 2, 3 and 4 contain comprehensive information on the model and its application.

Introductory Summary of the S Questions Model

There are four dimensions of questions in the S Questions Model:

- S1: Subject Matter Dimension of questions
- S2: Structure Dimension of questions
- S3: Seeking Information Dimension of questions
- S4: Shift Thinking Dimension of questions

S1: Subject Matter Dimension of Questions

All questions incorporate the S1: Subject Matter Dimension of questions and can be asked about the people involved in the conflict; the environment or context in which the conflict takes place; the problem or issue presented to mediation; and the interaction of the people, the environment and the problem.

S2: Structure Dimension of Questions

All questions have an S2: Structure Dimension of questions incorporated in them, in that an open or closed question may be chosen. After first deciding the subject matter and the structure of a question, the choice is then between asking an S3 Question or an S4 Question, or a combination of both.

S3: Seeking Information Dimension of Questions

A question from the S3: Seeking Information Dimension of questions is a simple linear question that clarifies existing information or introduces information that is either previously known, or is not already known, by each of the parties. An S3 question strategically targets the information that is required from the parties for the conversations that take place during a mediation process.

S4: Shift Thinking Dimension of Questions

Questions from the S4: Shift Thinking Dimension of questions are designed to uncover information that specifically creates new insight for the parties. The intention is to shift their thinking so that they look at the other party and their conflict in a different light. This is what is known as a paradigm shift.

While there are eight S4 questions and they are presented in the model in a certain order, each S4 question is a stand-alone question with its own unique purpose. Each S4 category of question may also be linked with each of the other seven categories of questions to achieve a specific outcome.

In general, the S4 questions move from hearing what happened and how a party interpreted it and acted upon it, to distilling and exploring the information presented, to making connections with other experiences or events. The questions help to identify any inner conflict or inconsistencies within a party, to safely teasing out alternative perspectives. They identify the core of a problem and facilitate the creation of a future without the problems of the past.

Premise on Which the S Questions Model Has Been Developed

The S Questions Model is designed on the premise that:

1. A paradigm shift may not be achieved by asking a simple linear question that looks for information, but a specific S4: Shift thinking question may be required.

2. The information that has formed the perspective and actions of a party may be deficient or distorted.

3. Parties approach their conflict based on their own subjective perspectives and that incisive questions need to be asked to facilitate them to look at their conflict, and their response to that conflict, from a different perspective.

4. Initial separate private meetings will take place between the mediator and each of the parties, both prior to bringing them together for a joint meeting and during a joint meeting, as needed.

5. To create safety, some of the questions in the model may need to be tested during the initial separate private meeting or in a private meeting during a joint session.

6. The decision to hold separate meetings during a joint meeting needs to be based on the needs of the mediation process and the parties, rather than on any specific model of mediation learned by the reader.

7. If a mediator inadvertently touches on a party's past trauma, then they need to slowly and gently name the fact that they have touched on it, acknowledge that it must have caused deep pain and then, after some seconds of quiet reflection, ask what needs to be in place so that the future for that party does not have the problems of the past.

Outline Summary of the S Questions Model

S1
Subject Matter Dimension of Questions
Choose the subject matter of the question:
People, Environment, Problem or PEP Interaction

S2
Structure Dimension of Questions
Open or Closed Questions
Do you want a simple yes or no answer, or do you need more information?

**Choose an S3 or S4 Question,
or a combination of an S3 and S4 Question**

S3
Seeking Information Dimension of Questions
Information gathering and clarifying existing information

S4
Shift Thinking Dimension of Questions
Exploring and Focusing Thinking Questions
Broadening and Expanding Thinking Questions

New information and insight leading to a paradigm shift

Figure: 1.1.

The S Questions Model

S1 — Subject Matter Dimension of Questions
Encompass the subject matter that is being discussed

People
The parties internal and external narratives, with their underlying interests and positions.

Environment
The environment in which the parties are operating (physical, social and psychological)

Problem
That which is presenting at mediation

PEP interaction
How the People, the Environment and the Problem interact, influence and impact on each other

S2 — Structure Dimension of Questions

The construction of a question can be phrased as an open question or a closed question.

Closed questions require a yes or no response.

Open questions are introduced with - Who? When? Where? Which? What? How? In what way? What if? If...?

Rarely use *Why* as it may be judgmental and result in the party needing to justify their actions.

S3 — Seeking Information Dimension of Questions
Information gathering questions about S1: Subject Matter Dimension of Questions, incorporating the People, Environment, and Problem (PEP) and PEP interaction

These questions clarify information given by parties and invite the parties' perspective on the conflict. They are a statement from the party's already held beliefs and opinions and form the pool of information about the conflict from which S4: Shift Thinking Dimension of Questions can be explored.

S4 — Shift Thinking Dimension of Questions
To uncover new information and insight, either by exploring and focusing thinking or by connecting and expanding thinking, leading to a paradigm shift

Journey of Inference Questions
Interpretations, Assumptions, Conclusions, Beliefs, Actions

Purpose: To identify the link between interpretations and actions. To explore parties' current narratives and to shift perspectives towards a new narrative.

Neuro-linguistic Programming (NLP) Based Questions
Deletions, Distortions, Generalizations

Purpose: To bring clarity, explore subjective realities, explore bias and misinterpretations, and create congruency in communication.

Distinctions and Differences Questions
People, Parts, Contexts, Opposites, Spatial, Comparisons, Time Span, Measurement or Ranking

Purpose: To bring clarity, relevance, measurement, boundary and a different perspective to the conflict.

Reflective Connecting Questions
Connecting with patterns and cycles of conflict, both intrapersonal and interpersonal, and in the broader context

Purpose: To raise awareness of negative patterns and cycles of conflict, to deconstruct past unhelpful patterns and to reconstruct new healthy patterns.

Cognitive Elements-based Questions
Knowledge; Opinion and Thinking; Beliefs, Values and Attitudes; Behaviour; Sense of Self/Identity; Environment

Purpose: To explore inner conflicts and inconsistencies between perception and reality, and between the six cognitive elements. To seek a paradigm shift that will restore cognitive consonance.

Other People Questions
Explore an imagined perspective of the other party, a third party, a cultural norm or hypothetical parties

Purpose: To open perspectives and create insight, safely.

Underlying Interests Questions
Conflict Triggers, Impact, Beliefs, Values and Attitudes

Purpose: To move from the conflict positions of the parties to the core of their conflict, and identify needs and underlying interests.

Future Focus Questions
Hypothetical, Conditional, Consequential, BATNA / MLATNA / WATNA

Purpose: To move parties off the conflict treadmill and facilitate cognitive thinking, leading to options and solutions.

Figure: 1.2.

The Purpose of Mediation Questions

The purpose of asking questions in mediation is to reveal new information and insight to parties in conflict so that a paradigm shift in their thinking and approach occurs. When parties present to mediation, they are usually holding an entrenched position that often presumes that the conflict is the fault of the other party and that the only way it can be solved is by the other party changing their position or behavior.

Each party creates their conflict case based on their own unique perspectives, interpretations and subjective realities. This makes it inevitable that parties will hold an entrenched position and may not understand the perspective or position of the other. Hence the importance of asking exploratory and incisive questions to bring new information to the mediation process, and to gently challenge the perspectives of each of the parties. This is how parties can gain new insight that leads to a paradigm shift in their perspective.

Paradigm and Perspective

A paradigm is how we see, interpret and understand our world, and our role in it, and how we understand the roles of others. It is our view of the world and how it should be, and our model or template from which we make sense of our world.

Our individual and unique paradigm is our reference point for interpreting information and giving meaning to what happens in it. It is a way of organizing, classifying and condensing sensory information to help us to understand our world.

The Formation of Our Paradigm

Our paradigm has been uniquely customized in line with:

- The beliefs and values that we developed from our experiences during our formation, about ourselves, others and our world; and
- The experiences of the significant others in our lives and how their values and beliefs were portrayed to us and internalized by us; and
- Our culture, education, religion, race and any other condtioning influence that contributed to us being who we are.

Perspectives

Our paradigm influences our perspectives which, in turn, filter incoming information, so that we see and experience our world in the way we expect to see and experience it, according to our paradigm. Our filters are conditioned by our experiences as we learn about our surroundings throughout our lives. Paradigms often limit and color our perceptions and awareness, resulting in us finding it hard to see something that does not conform to our basic assumptions.

It is important to note that stored memories are memories of our perceptions or subjective realities, *not* memories of reality.

> We see the world, not as it is, but as we are — or, as we are conditioned to see it.
>
> — Stephen R. Covey, *The 7 Habits of Highly Effective People: Powerful Lessons in Personal Change* [1]

Paradigm Shift

A paradigm shift is when we change our thinking, perspective and understanding about a situation. In mediation, this can result in a change in our approach to the conflict and our response to it.

Example of a Paradigm Shift

In his book *The 7 Habits of Highly Effective People*, Stephen Covey [2] describes experiencing a paradigm shift in his thinking and approach:

> I remember a mini-paradigm shift I experienced one morning on a subway in New York. People were sitting quietly — some reading newspapers, some lost in thought, some resting with their eyes closed. It was a calm, peaceful scene. Then suddenly, a man and his children entered the subway. The children were so loud and rambunctious that instantly the whole climate changed. The man sat down next to me and closed his eyes, apparently oblivious to the situation. The children were yelling back and forth, throwing things, even grabbing people's papers. It was very disturbing. And yet, the man sitting next to me did nothing.
>
> It was difficult not to feel irritated. I could not believe that he could be so insensitive as to let his children run wild like that and do nothing about it, taking no responsibility at all. It was easy to see that everyone else on the subway felt irritated, too.
>
> So finally, with what I felt was unusual patience and restraint, I turned to him and said, "Sir, your children are really disturbing a lot of people. I wonder if you couldn't control them a little more?" The

man lifted his gaze as if to come to a consciousness of the situation for the first time and said softly, "Oh, you're right. I guess I should do something about it. We just came from the hospital where their mother died about an hour ago, I don't know what to think, and I guess they don't know how to handle it either."

Can you imagine what I felt at that moment? My paradigm shifted. Suddenly I saw things differently, and because I saw differently, I thought differently, I felt differently, I behaved differently. My irritation vanished. I didn't have to worry about controlling my attitude or my behavior; my heart was filled with the man's pain. Feelings of sympathy and compassion flowed freely. "Your wife just died? Oh, I'm so sorry! Can you tell me about it? What can I do to help?" Everything changed in an instant.

The positive aspect illustrated by this story is that our created paradigm, or our view of our world, along with our patterns of behavior, are not rigid, but are open to change. By gently listening and reflecting back to a party what you have heard them say and asking insightful questions, a mediator can provide a safe space for parties to reflect on their paradigm and perceptions, look at their conflicts differently and make changes to their behavior if they choose to do so. A mediator's role is to work with the entrenched perspectives and positions of parties to achieve a shift in their thinking and their approach to their conflict. The S4 Shift Thinking questions in the S Questions Model are designed to shift the thinking and perceptions of parties in conflict.

Figure 1.3.
Paradigm Shift
CREDIT: O'SULLIVAN SOLUTIONS

How We Process and
Communicate Information

How Information Is Processed

T HIS CHAPTER EXAMINES SOME OF THE FACTORS that result in the deletion
and distortion of the information absorbed by our brain at a conscious
level, and how we also delete and distort information when we communicate
to others.

Neuro-linguistic Programming

Richard Bandler and John Grinder are the cofounders of Neuro-linguistic
Programming (NLP)[3], a methodology to understand patterns of human
behavior.

Robert Dilts describes NLP as encompassing the three most influential
components involved in producing human experience: neurology, language
and programming. The neurological system regulates how our bodies function,
language determines how we interact and communicate with other people, and
our programming determines the kinds of models of the world we create. In
other words, NLP describes the fundamental dynamics between mind (neuro),
language (linguistic) and how their interplay affects our body and behavior
(programming).

Bandler and Grinder state that we interact with our world using our five
senses: visual (images), auditory (sounds), kinesthetic (touch and internal
feelings) and, to a lesser extent, gustatory (tastes) and olfactory (smells). The
entirety of our experience is represented (re-presented) to our brain in sensorial
terms, and we rely on our senses again to recall this experience.

For example, when we are at a barbecue with friends, we see ourselves and
our friends, we hear the laughter of our friends, we feel the warmth of the sun
on our back, we smell the meat cooking and we taste the delicious food. When
we recall the memory of this event and retell this experience to others, we rely
on our senses to do so as well.

We know that our five senses are the channels through which we absorb
information and re-present our experiences to our brain, and that the information that we absorb is influenced by our uniquely created filters. We now need
to look briefly at the factors that influence the amount and type of information
that we absorb, and how the emotions that surface for us when we are absorbing information can influence how we interpret that information as well.

Factors That Contribute to the Information That We Process

The deletion and distortion of the information we absorb is influenced by:

1. The amount of information that is absorbed by our conscious mind
2. The type of information that is absorbed and processed by our conscious mind
3. The emotions that surface for us when we are processing and interpreting incoming information

1. The Amount *of Information That Is Absorbed by Our Conscious Mind*

Our senses re-present to our brain 11 million bits of information per second from our environment for processing, but our conscious mind is only able to process approximately 40 bits per second.

> The fact is that every single second, millions of bits of information flood in through our senses. But our consciousness processes only perhaps 40 bits per second — at most. Millions and millions of bits are condensed to a conscious experience that contains practically no information at all. Every single second, every one of us discards millions of bits in order to arrive at the special state known as consciousness.
>
> — Torr Norretranders, *The User Illusion: Cutting Consciousness Down to Size*, Penguin Press, 1999

In his book, Norretranders quotes Professor Manfred Zimmermann from the Institute of Physiology at Heidelberg University:

> We can therefore conclude that the maximal information flow of the process of conscious sensory perception is about 40 bits per second — many orders of magnitude below that taken in by receptors (nerve endings). Our perception, then, would appear to be limited to a minute part of the abundance of information available as sensory input.

Having looked at the limited *amount* of information that our brain or conscious mind absorbs, we will now look at how our unique paradigm and perspective influences the *type* of information or data we absorb.

2. The Type of Information That Is Absorbed and Processed by Our Conscious Mind

As described in Chapter 1, the type of information we absorb is limited to that which matches our paradigm. The filters through which we absorb and interpret our world are uniquely customized by us and are based on the beliefs and values we developed during our formation, how these were modeled to us by the significant people in our lives, our culture and educational experiences, and any other experiences that helped create our perspective.

Factors That Contribute to the Type of Information Represented to Our Brain

SELECTIVE ATTENTIONAL BLINDNESS

While our paradigm and perspective may influence us to only focus on the things we wish to focus on, the problem is that when we specifically focus on one thing, we can easily overlook something else. This was demonstrated in an experiment called the Selective Attention Test undertaken by Simons and Chabris in 1999. [4]

The experiment [5] involved several people standing in a circle and passing a ball to each other. Viewers were asked to count the number of times the players wearing white T-shirts passed the ball. In the middle of this exercise, a person dressed as a very large gorilla walked into the center of the circle, turned to the camera, pounded their chest and walked away. The experiment showed that more than 50 percent of viewers were so focused on counting the number of ball passes that they completely missed the gorilla. From my own experience during the delivery of mediation or conflict training, I would put the percentage at more than 50 percent. In one case that I observed, only 5 participants in a group of 39 noticed the gorilla, and only a small percentage got the correct answer to the question of how many times the players in the white T-shirts passed the ball.

CHANGE BLINDNESS

Simons and Chabris also carried out an experiment called the Door Study. [6] This demonstrated that we sometimes fail to detect large changes to objects and scenes because our mind tends to fixate on the first image we see.

In this study, a researcher asked a stranger in the street for directions. Two workers who were part of the experiment walked down the street holding a door and carried it between the two people who were conversing. As the door passed between them, both the researcher and the stranger found their vision of each other being momentarily interrupted. During this interruption, the researcher was replaced by one of the workers carrying the door. In follow-up research questions, many of the people who had taken part in the experiment had not noticed the change, and if they had noticed, did not seem to be concerned that they were suddenly talking to a different person.

BIASED ASSIMILATION

Biased Assimilation is when we focus only on what we want to see or hear because it affirms our perspective and paradigm. However, we also tend to see and hear only that on which we are focused, as evidenced in the Selective Attentional Blindness study experiment, so this becomes a never-ending cycle of distorted and deleted information intake.

In "Biased Assimilation and Attitude Polarization: The Effects of Prior Theories on Subsequently Considered Evidence," Charles G. Lord, Lee Ross and Mark R. Lepper of Stanford University state that:

> People who hold strong opinions on complex social issues are likely to examine relevant empirical evidence in a biased manner. They are apt to accept "confirming" evidence at face value while subjecting "disconfirming" evidence to critical evaluation, and, thus draw undue support for their initial positions from mixed or random empirical findings.

Similarly, parties engaging in mediation enter the process with their narrative firmly in place. Prior to mediation, they are more likely to have only listened to people or information that confirmed their narrative and position.

COGNITIVE DISSONANCE

This bias refers to the fact that it is psychologically uncomfortable for most people to consider data that contradicts their viewpoint. This is covered in more detail in Chapter 14.

FALSE CONSENSUS BIAS

People can be of the view that their opinions, beliefs and values are normal and typical of other people. They assume that others also think the same way they do and, as a result, only look for the type of information that confirms their view.

REACTIVE DEVALUATION

People tend to minimize the value of a statement or action by another party due to concerns about the credibility or competence of the source.

ATTRIBUTIONAL BIAS

This bias refers to a person's tendency to be antagonistic to an enemy and assume negative intent toward that person, even in the absence of any evidence. This affects the type of information that they absorb.

Having looked at the limited *amount* of information our brain takes in, and at how our unique perspective and paradigm influences the *type* of information or data we absorb, we will now look at how the *emotions* that surface for us while we interpret that incoming information also affect the information we absorb.

3. The Emotions *That Surface for Us When We Are Processing and Interpreting Information*

The amount and type of information we take in is further influenced by the emotions we feel while we absorb this information. During an event, if the social stimuli experienced by a person are negative and create fear, then biological hardwiring, governed by memories of past negative stimuli, will activate a threat response in the brain. It is important to note again that the memories stored by our brain are merely memories of our perceptions or subjective realities.

Jeremy Lack [8] maintains that our perceptions are influenced by our emotions and therefore subjective. If we are lacking in emotional self-awareness or emotional intelligence, then the emotional memories of our perceptions will influence the interpretation of information presented to us, and this may result in our becoming illogical in our thinking.

In conclusion, there is a staggering amount of information available to us that we do not process at a conscious level. This highlights the need for a mediator to ask strategic, incisive and effective questions during mediation discussions, to create clarity of thinking and ensure that deeper information is uncovered.

The NLP Model of Communication

The NLP model of communication is a useful tool for understanding how we process incoming information through our uniquely created filters. NLP theory [7] shows that, consciously or unconsciously, we delete, distort and generalize our experiences in line with our paradigm. In NLP terminology, our paradigm is referred to as our world map. We perform these mental manipulations to ensure that our world map remains intact and matches our created paradigm, reinterpreting information so that it becomes distorted and generalized and editing or deleting information that is not in line with our paradigm.

We perform these deletions, distortions and generalizations of sensory information via subjective, customized filters. The result is that the information we present to our brains at the end of this process can vary greatly from the information that was initially available to us.

This concept of deletion, distortion and generalization of incoming information is explored using the NLP Meta Model, described in detail in the following table.

The NLP Meta Model — Deletions, Distortions and Generalizations

Deletions	
Deletions occur when we only pay attention to certain aspects of the information presented to us through our senses. We absorb the information that affirms our paradigm and filter out any information that we either do	not think is relevant or did not see in the first place. The deletion process is often unconscious and can result in important information not being known to the parties in conflict or not voiced in a mediation process.

Distortions	
Distortions happen when we change our experience of something by unconsciously altering the way in which we absorb information and relay it to others. We may blow something completely out of proportion or else diminish it; we may also alter the sequence of events or make assumptions about them and jump to conclusions. We may even think that we can mind read and assume someone else's state, but all of this is only based on our own biased and selective assumptions, and not on our ability to mind read!	For example, when someone says,"I know exactly why she did that!" If our perceptions are based on the information we absorb, and if we have already deleted or distorted some of that information, then our experience will only be based on the remaining information absorbed. This will result in even further distortion of the information we process at a conscious level. An example of how this happens can be found in Chapter 10.

Generalizations	
Generalizations occur when we take a specific experience, draw universal assumptions about it, then apply it as true to everything outside the context of that specific experience. For example, we can have an opinion of one person and then apply it to a whole category or race of people: "You can never trust anyone from that race — they are all criminals."	When generalizing, we use words such as *everyone, all, no one, never* and *always*. Generalizing gives us a way of predicting the world based on what we have experienced previously. We then expect that our future will fit into this previous pattern and only look for information that confirms our expectations.

Our Created Paradigm Becomes Our Reference Point for Interpreting Information

If we did not delete, distort and generalize the information absorbed into our brain, our neurology would not be able to cope with the information overload. However, the result is that the information that we do absorb is not an accurate reflection of what happened. With such limited information from which to draw conclusions, no two people will have the same response or reaction, despite having been exposed to the same stimuli.

> We need something that prevents our brain from over-loading and keeps us sane. Luckily there is a part of our brain located between the conscious mind and the unconscious mind that filters out much of this information. This small filter is called the Reticular Activating System, and it helps to keep us sane by looking for information in the outside world that matches the beliefs already stored in the unconscious mind.
>
> — *Train Your Brain*, Dana Wilde, Balboa Press, 2013

Our uniquely customized paradigm becomes our reference point about who we are, what our status is, what we are certain about, what we think is right or wrong, how things were in the past, how things should be in the future, how we make decisions, what makes us comfortable, what we consider to be fair and what will influence what we communicate to others. Any interpretations or assumptions that we make may be based on the incomplete and distorted information that we process at a conscious level, and these assumptions are influenced by our own uniquely customized paradigm. While we can share experiences, our understanding, perspective, interpretation and assumptions of an experience are subjective, and therefore different to those who may have shared that experience with us.

> Two people can see the same thing, disagree, and yet both be right. It's not logical; it's psychological.
>
> — Stephen R. Covey,
> *The 7 Habits of Highly Effective People*[9]

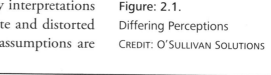

Figure: 2.1.
Differing Perceptions
CREDIT: O'SULLIVAN SOLUTIONS

How We Communicate Information to Others

After an experience or situation, we are left with our perception of what happened. This perception is what we re-present to ourselves, what we react to or act on and what we re-present to others, both consciously and unconsciously.

When we communicate to another person, we make assumptions about what they already know or do not know, and about how they will perceive what is being said. Therefore, when we communicate to them, we consciously or unconsciously delete, distort or generalize the information we impart. When others communicate with us, they also delete, distort or generalize the information they impart to us.

> NLP suggests that we delete, generalize and distort our experiences when we transform them into internal representations (re-presenting the experiences in the brain). Then our choice of words to describe those experiences deletes, generalizes and distorts it all over again.
>
> — Joseph O'Connor, *NLP Workbook: A Practical Guide to Achieving the Results You Want* [10]

Distortion, Deletion and Generalization When Communicating to Others

The process by which we limit and distort our representation of our world to ourselves is the same as that by which we limit and distort our communication of our world to others.

For example, if we must decide whether to rent a small, cheap apartment or a large, expensive one, and we really want the larger apartment, we may only see the negatives in the smaller apartment option and the positives in the larger option. Moreover, when we start looking for advice, we may only ask our wealthier friends and may frame our questions in a way that will give us the response we want:

"There is a wonderful large apartment in the city that I am thinking of renting and it would really suit me, and there is also a smaller, cheaper one there too, what do you think I should do?"

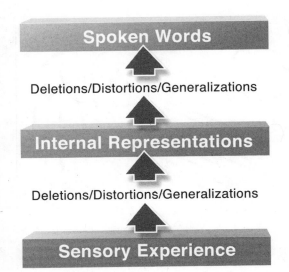

Figure: 2.2. NLP — Sensory Experience to Spoken Words
CREDIT: O'SULLIVAN SOLUTIONS

The Language Structures We Use When We Communicate with Others

In *NLP Workbook*, Joseph O'Connor[11] states that we use two levels of language:

1. Surface Structure Language
2. Deep Structure Language

Surface Structure Language

These are the things that we say to ourselves and to other people. The surface structure of our language cannot contain everything that is in the deep structure so we delete, distort and generalize some aspects of our communication, both to others and to ourselves.

> Example of surface structure language:
>
> He never takes me to dinner anymore like all other men do with their wives! This is not fair and I want it to change.

Deep Structure Language

If we were to look below the surface structure language level for underlying needs and interests, we would hear a very different narrative.

> Example of deep structure language:
>
> He never takes me to dinner anymore and this must mean that he has stopped loving me, so that must mean that I must be unlovable.

This latter narrative can be the underlying meaning of what we say. It comprises everything we know about an experience. But we either do not express it when we communicate with another person, or do not know it consciously.[12]

During mediation, the parties usually present a surface level of communication before the mediator starts asking questions to uncover their deeper levels of concern and underlying interests. While a party's presenting issues and positions are conscious, the many unseen layers of needs and interests below the surface can be either conscious or unconscious. Much of our information or data processing, including what we delete, distort and generalize, is accomplished outside our conscious awareness, and most of the brain's activity takes place outside our direct conscious control.

How we communicate to ourselves and to others indicates how vital it is that a mediator seeks to clarify existing information and bring new information into a mediation process to minimize the effects of information deletion, distortion and generalization. Questions need to focus on the deep structure language level so that underlying interests and needs are uncovered. This is what will create understanding between the parties. Chapter 16 includes a type of S4 question called Underlying Interests and comprehensively demonstrates how to reach the deeper-structure language levels or underlying interests of parties in conflict.

> Between what I think, what I wish to say, what I think I am saying, what I actually say, and what you wish to hear, what you actually hear, and what you understand.... There are 10 reasons why we may have difficulty communicating, but let's try anyway.
>
> — Bernard Werber [13]

Using Mediation Questions to Create a Paradigm Shift

The questions asked of a party in mediation should lead them to readjust their subjective reality and perspective. The assumption is that if subjective realities shape behavior, then readjusting them might lead to a paradigm shift in a party's thinking and therefore a readjustment of their behaviors. A mediator needs to support parties to think about their thinking as this is what influences their subjective realities and their actions and reactions.

In her book *NLP at Work,* [14] Sue Knight explains what is needed to support people to think clearly:

> Once you have experienced something, it becomes a memory. When you react to a memory you are reacting to the way you store that memory. Supporting a party to think clearly and to make distinctions in their thinking helps them to change the way they are storing that memory so that they can start to feel the way they would like to feel.

When parties shift their thinking, their changed perspectives will result in changed behavior. The role of the mediator is to explore the unique perception or paradigm of each of the parties. A mediator needs to be mindful, present and skillful in understanding the experience of others. Then they need to work with those experiences, rather than with their own interpretations of a party's experience.

A shift in thinking and paradigm is achieved by asking questions that:

1. Bring clarity to the parties' thinking
2. Uncover unknown information
3. Focus and explore the parties' thinking
4. Broaden and expand the parties' thinking
5. Create new insights

This is what S4: Shift Thinking questions do. So, ask lots and lots of S4 questions!

Hazard Warning

Asking questions that reshape people's perceptions and memories should not be a direct goal in itself as this would be highly unethical in a mediation process. Instead, questions need to be asked that will facilitate parties to gain new information and deeper insight so that they can be conscious and self-determining about their choices and decisions.

Key Learning

- We take in information via our five senses — visual (images), auditory (sounds), kinesthetic (touch and internal feelings), gustatory (tastes) and olfactory (smells).

- The information we absorb is determined by the amount of information our brain absorbs, the type of information we absorb and by the emotions that surface for us when we are interpreting and absorbing that information.

- While our senses absorb and re-present to our brain 11 million bits of information per second from our environment for processing, our conscious mind processes only 40 bits of information per second.

- Our paradigm, or how we see and interpret the world, has been uniquely customized in line with our past experiences, our values and the beliefs we have formed about ourselves, others and our world. We create our own unique filters for interpreting incoming information about our world, our role in it and the roles of others.

- Our paradigm informs and influences how we file every piece of data absorbed by our brain, and this results in our interpreting a situation from our own unique, subjective reference points.

- Our stored memories are only memories of our perceptions — they are not memories of reality.

- We limit and distort our representation of our world to ourselves. The process by which we do this is the same process as that by which we limit and distort our expression of our world to others.

- A mediator needs to bring consciousness to the subjective interpretations of the parties rather than working with the positional data presented by them in mediation. It is this that enables a party to gain a new perspective and experience a paradigm shift.

- The purpose for asking questions in mediation is to uncover new information, clarify existing information and facilitate a party in conflict to gain deeper insight and achieve a paradigm shift in their perspective, thinking and approach.

- There is a need to ask lots and lots of S4: Shift Thinking questions to bring more information into the mediation process.

Working with the Brain in Mediation

The Brain

THIS CHAPTER PRESENTS AN OUTLINE of how we are biologically hardwired, and the implications of this learning for working safely with parties in mediation. It outlines the basic functions of each part of the brain and specifically the ways in which parties become stressed in conflict or during mediation.

> No area of understanding is more relevant and important to mediation competency than a basic understanding of how the human brain functions, perceives events, processes emotional notions, cognitive response and formulates decisions. The awareness of cognitive neuroscience and psychology are at the heart of our work in managing conflict and problem solving.
>
> — Robert Benjamin [15]

The theories and concepts in this chapter form the basis of the methodology that needs to be employed for asking questions using the S Questions Model.

The Evolution-formed Triune Brain

The physician and neuroscientist Paul D. MacLean [16] states that the human brain has evolved into three independent, but interconnected, layers of brain matter referred to as the triune brain. These layers of distinct evolution are known as the reptilian brain, the midbrain or limbic system and the frontal brain or neocortex.

Figure 3.1: The Evolution-formed Triune Brain
CREDIT: O'SULLIVAN SOLUTIONS

The Reptilian Brain

This is the most primitive part of the human brain that started to evolve more than five hundred million years ago. It is the location of the instinctive survival reflexes. The reptilian brain regulates functions such as digestion, circulation, breathing and heart rate, any of which can be affected if we feel threatened.

The Limbic System (Midbrain)

This is the second layer of the brain. It contains the amygdala and is believed to be the part of the brain where information from the senses (sight, sound, touch, smell and taste) is first processed. Here is where our emotions are generated as a first

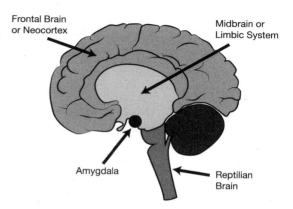

reaction to any stimulus from the senses and where our unconscious memories, including our emotional memories, are stored.

The amygdala is our threat detector. It calculates whether a stimulus is to be feared and avoided, or whether something is a reward and can be approached. The amygdala's evaluation of the stimulus, with reference points to past experiences and memories of perceptions, determines the conscious experience of our feelings. In the past, the presence of a wild animal represented real danger, but today's threats are less clearly defined, and therefore more complex.

The amygdala processes information from our five senses and from our memory. If no memory of any threatening significance is evoked, then the information travels on to the frontal brain (neocortex).

The Frontal Brain (Neocortex)

Conscious memory and high-order cognitive thinking take place in this layer of the brain. It controls higher functions such as language, logic, reasoning and creativity.

When we are highly stressed, the functions of the frontal brain disconnect due to the negative impact of stress hormones on the hippocampus. The hippocampus is a small organ that forms an important part of the limbic system, which regulates emotions. The hippocampus is associated mainly with memory, particularly long-term memory, which includes all past knowledge and experience.

Because stress hormones have a negative effect on the hippocampus, a flood of them leaves us in an emotionally charged state, without input from the cognitive thinking brain. We may start to think and act irrationally, but the extent to which this happens depends on our level of emotional intelligence.

We will now turn to the physiological process that occurs when we have a sudden, strong emotional reaction to a stimulus.

The Nervous System and the Amygdala

Amygdala hijack [18] is the term used to describe a sudden and disproportionate emotional reaction to a stimulus that has evoked a strong emotional memory from our past. A part of the limbic system, the amygdala is the emotional center of the brain and reflects our fundamental needs. It can produce split-second responses when we feel threatened. We experience a sudden and disproportionate emotional reaction to a stimulus when someone else's values, needs, interests, beliefs, assumptions or perceptions may seem incompatible with ours. This stimulus may evoke a fearful response in us. The more emotionally intelligent and self-aware we are, the easier it is for us to regulate our emotions and access our rational brain during conflict. But if we are unable to do this effectively, we will enter the grip of an amygdala hijack and be unable to access our frontal cognitive thinking brain until we have calmed down.

Amygdala Hijack

Our perception of our world occurs via our five senses.[19] Information from these senses enters our brain stem from the spinal cord and travels along neural pathways to the limbic system. When our senses perceive a threat, our sympathetic nervous system is stimulated, resulting in a fight or flight response, also known as a stress response. When this happens, we are no longer able to think rationally. Instead, we are in reaction mode.

↓

When a threat is perceived, emotional memories stored in the midbrain's amygdala can be evoked.

↓

When the amygdala is stimulated by a perceived threat, it signals to the hypothalamus, and this results in the release of the stress hormones cortisol and adrenaline. These hormones are released into the bloodstream and transported to the brain, where they disconnect the frontal lobes and leave us at the mercy of our emotions and caught in amygdala hijack. This is a strong emotional state.

Amygdala Hijack

The oxygen and glucose necessary for effective frontal brain high-order thinking are then diverted to the amygdala in the limbic system to process these emotions. While this takes place, the frontal brain is deprived of oxygen and glucose and unable to function effectively at a rational level.

↓

Emotional self-regulation[20] activates the parasympathetic nervous system, which is responsible for the release of hormones into the bloodstream to act as antidotes to the stress hormones.

↓

These antidotes gradually slow breathing and reduce the heart rate, enabling oxygen and glucose to return to the frontal brain, which permits rational thinking to take place again.

When an amygdala hijack occurs, this indicates that something that is of fundamental value to a person is perceived by them to be under threat. This emotional response to a stimulus, and the triggering event that caused it, needs to be explored to give parties in mediation an opportunity to talk effectively about their issues and their accompanying emotions.

It is only after this has been done that discussions can move on to exploring options for solution. If a party is asked about possible solutions when they are in the grip of an amygdala hijack (and so in a highly emotional state), they may be unable to give an effective cognitive response.

From a neurological perspective, the role of a mediator may be described as minimizing perceptions of danger enabling cognitive appreciations of emotions, dampening the amygdala and helping parties to self-regulate.

— Jeremy Lack and Francois Bogacz [21]

Biological Hardwiring

David Rock has written many of the central academic and discussion papers that have defined the field of neuroleadership. [22] His social neuroscience theory explores the biological foundations of the way people relate to each other and to themselves. Rock states that two themes are emerging from studies of social neuroscience:

- Firstly, that much of what motivates and drives our social behavior is governed by an overarching organizing principle of minimizing threat and maximizing reward. [23]
- Secondly, that several domains of social experience draw upon the same brain networks used for primary survival needs.

Rock suggests that human beings may be hardwired evolutionarily and may have been created to respond to ten neuro-commandments that encompass the need to minimize threat, maximize reward and have our emotions regulated.

Ten Neuro-commandments

1. Thou shalt avoid pain and seek reward
2. Thou shalt be more sensitive to danger or fear than to reward
3. Thou shalt regulate your emotions
4. Thou shalt operate cognitively in two gears
5. Thy social stimuli shalt be as powerful as thy physical ones
6. Thou shalt seek comfortable status positions
7. Thou shalt always predict to have a sense of certainty
8. Thou shalt retain your autonomy
9. Thou shalt relate to others
10. Thou shalt prefer fair behavior

Rock maintains that neuro-commandments 1 to 5 encompass the need to minimize threat, maximize reward and have our emotions regulated, while neuro-commandments 6 to 10 encompass the SCARF® Drivers: status; certainty; autonomy; relatedness (being connected to and similar and secure with others); and being treated fairly. [24]

Rock states that these SCARF® Drivers are treated in the brain in much the same way as our primary needs for physical safety, food, water and shelter are. Unfulfilled SCARF® Drivers have the same impact on the brain as a physical threat and may result in an amygdala hijack.

Let us now look at each of the neuro-commandments individually.

Neuro-commandment 1: Thou shalt avoid pain and seek reward

Humans are driven to minimize or avoid pain, and to maximize reward. If there is a sense that they are in danger or are afraid, resulting from a negative triggering event, then biological hardwiring, governed by memories of stimuli, will trigger an avoid-threat reflex. If a threat is detected, the sympathetic nervous system is stimulated and prepares to meet that stressful situation, resulting in a fight or flight response, as necessary. If a person senses a reward, they will unconsciously and automatically display an approach-reward reflex.

Neuro-commandment 2: Thou shalt be more sensitive to danger or fear than to reward

The avoid-threat reflex is far stronger and longer lasting than the approach-reward reflex. While this is a protective mechanism, it leads to our inability to think cognitively and clearly when we are in a negative emotional state.

Neuro-commandment 3: Thou shalt regulate your emotions

When the amygdala is activated, it draws resources of oxygen and glucose from the frontal brain, which is then left without its necessary resources to perform cognitive thinking. It is through conscious awareness and the development of social and emotional intelligence that self-regulation can take place. This then leads to our ability to cognitively assess a social stimulus so that scripted patterns of behavior are overcome.

Neuro-commandment 4: Thou shalt operate cognitively in two gears

When parties in conflict are emotional, they react and act on auto-pilot or default mode. This is referred to as the X-system, as proposed by Matthew D. Lieberman [25] and quoted by Jeremy Lack and Francois Bogacz in their paper "The Neurophysiology of ADR and Process Design: A New Approach to Conflict Prevention and Resolution?": [26]

> Human beings have two basic modes of functioning:
>
> - The first is called the "reflexive mode" which is regulated by neural assemblies in the brain known as the "X-system." This system relies primarily on patterns to make unconscious predictions, and on cognitive reflexes. This is the auto-pilot state of immediate and unconscious reaction that we function in most of the time.
> - The second mode is called the "reflective mode," and it is the responding mode that is regulated by a different neural assembly system called the "C-system." This is the considered and measured response that comes from those with emotional intelligence.

Neuro-commandment 5: Thy social stimuli shalt be as powerful as thy physical ones

When we receive negative social stimuli that engender a feeling of fear or threat, such as during exclusion, bullying or rejection, this activates the same networks in the brain as those activated by physical pain.

Neuro-commandments 6–10:

While neuro-commandments 1–5 ensure primary survival, we are also programmed to ensure social survival. David Rock says it is important to recognize that human beings have specific SCARF® Drivers and that a threat to any one of them can engender an emotional reaction and activate the accompanying avoid-threat reflex.

- The avoid-threat reflex is caused by us experiencing a sense of danger or pain.
- The approach-reward reflex is caused by us experiencing reward and pleasure.

Rock states that we make such decisions about threat or reward, based on our emotional response, five times every second. This is a very subtle process, and we are making decisions about everything, good or bad, all the time.

Rock's SCARF® Drivers Model [27] provides a framework to capture the common factors that can activate a reward or threat response in social situations. The five domains in the model activate either the "primary reward" or "primary threat" circuitry (and associated networks) of the brain. For example, neuroscience has demonstrated that a perceived threat to one's status activates similar brain networks to a threat to one's life. In the same way, a perceived increase in fairness activates the same reward circuitry as a perceived monetary reward.

SCARF® Drivers Model

The five SCARF® Drivers — status, certainty, autonomy, relatedness and fairness — provide an effective tool for exploring how parties in conflict perceive and respond to social situations. To different degrees, impacts on all five domains can influence a person's perception of a situation and whether they view it as being threatening or rewarding. The needs of people in conflict, and the impact of the conflict on them, can be explored by using the five domains as subjects for exploratory questioning. This is covered in Chapter 16.

The Five SCARF® Drivers

STATUS: OUR SENSE OF IMPORTANCE RELATIVE TO OTHERS

The perception of a reduction in status, or an actual reduction in status, can generate a strong threat response in us. In conflicts presenting to mediation, it is quite common for one party or both parties to have an underlying need to have their reputation or status restored. We generate a slight reward response when we perceive that our status has risen, but the threat response we generate when we perceive that our status has fallen is much stronger. Research has illustrated that, within the same subjects, an experience of social rejection and an experience of physical pain activated overlapping neural regions. Experiences of both physical and social pain rely on shared neural substrates. [28]

CERTAINTY: OUR NEED TO BE ABLE TO MAKE ACCURATE PREDICTIONS ABOUT OUR FUTURE

The brain is a pattern-recognition machine that is constantly trying to predict the future based on past experiences. Increased ambiguity or uncertainty decreases activation in reward circuits and increases activation in the threat neural circuitry, for instance in the amygdala. When one or more parties have unrealized expectations of the other, or when organizational change takes place, this can be a contributing factor to a conflict presenting to mediation.

AUTONOMY: OUR FUNDAMENTAL NEED TO HAVE PERSONAL CONTROL AND SELF-DETERMINATION OVER THE EVENTS IN OUR LIVES

In a study by Leotti and Delgado,[29] the anticipation of making a choice demonstrated increased activity in the reward regions of the brain. Mediation cases in the workplace can often revolve around unclear job descriptions or a supervisor's micro-management of an employee, and these can affect a person's sense of autonomy. The social need for autonomy can arise in all sectors of mediation practice.

RELATEDNESS: THE DEGREE TO WHICH WE FEEL A SENSE OF CONNECTEDNESS, SIMILARITY AND SAFETY WITH THOSE AROUND US

This is directly related to whether we feel that we are engaging in safe or threatening social interactions. The phenomena known as "in-group preference" or "out-group bias" refers to the consistent finding that we feel greater trust and empathy toward those who are like us and are part of the same social circles and we feel greater distrust and reduced empathy toward those who we perceive as dissimilar to us, or who are members of other social groups. The definition of in-group and out-group members is not limited to racial, ethnic, religious or political distinctions, but can be seen where a person feels marginalized through bullying or harassment at work or feels excluded in a social or community setting.

FAIRNESS: OUR FEELING THAT WE ARE TREATED IN AN IMPARTIAL, EQUAL AND JUST MANNER, WITHOUT FAVORITISM OR DISCRIMINATION

The perception of fairness is very important to us in any situation. We do not base this perception on cold or rational thought processes, because emotions are integral to our judgment of fairness. The types of judgment we make evolve over time through our social experiences with others. [30] Recent research has shown that the amygdala is activated during the rejection of unfair offers and that receiving or making fair offers activates a reward response. In mediation, the perception or actuality of fair treatment can often be the underlying interest of a party — for example, in civil and commercial mediations.

THE INTERRELATION BETWEEN THE FIVE DOMAINS OF THE SCARF® DRIVERS MODEL

There are several ways in which the five domains of social experience relate to one another, and how the SCARF® Drivers are impacted will depend on every party's unique perceptions.

Example:

Experiencing redundancy

> When a person is made redundant from work, all five domains of the SCARF® Drivers Model may be affected. Every individual's reaction to this event will depend on how they perceive their world, which will affect whether they sense redundancy as a threat or a reward.

Perspective of Person A

If Person A feels their status is defined by their job, if he no longer has certainty about his economic survival and if he feels he will lose his autonomy over his earning capacity, he will register an avoid-threat reflex. If he also misses the company of his workmates because he was part of that workforce all of his working life (relatedness), and if he feels that being made redundant is unfair as he personally did nothing to affect the downturn in the economy and its impact on the company, then he will feel negatively affected by the loss of his job.

Perspective of Person B

On the other hand, Person B may perceive the situation completely differently and may be delighted that from now on she can make her own decision (autonomy) about when she gets out of bed in the morning and what she will plan for her day. She may have been counting the years to retirement because she wanted to spend more time with her partner (relatedness) and become better at tennis and beat her friend who is always boasting about her game (status). She may never have liked working in a team with ten others and may have felt stressed because she was never able to forecast accurately how her boss would react to her work output, or even what mood her boss would be in (certainty), and she thinks that the redundancy package that he is being offered is very fair.

When the SCARF® Drivers are activated, parties in conflict feel threatened or rewarded, and this has an impact on their perception of the social situation in which they find themselves. Whether a party in mediation is moved by an approach-reward or avoid-threat reflex will influence their ability to think cognitively and make rational decisions.

> In the face of conflict there is no such thing as a cool-headed reasoner. We, in conflict situations, feel and act like prey animals; who have a natural, psycho-biological discomfort and unease about being in foreign terrain and in a circumstance over which we do not have complete control. At worst, we have abject fear of being compromised or injured.
>
> — Antonio Damasio, Van Allen Professor and
> Head of Neurology at the University of Iowa

Working with the Avoid-threat Reflex in Mediation

This section outlines the need to work with parties' avoid-threat reflex as a means to reach their underlying needs and interests. Parties in conflict experience a wide range of emotions when they come to mediation: tension, anxiety, fear, embarrassment, uncertainty or worry. Sitting in the same room as the person with whom they are in conflict will probably elicit many other feelings such as anger, frustration, vengefulness, distrust, bitterness, hurt, sadness or regret.

> When fear is aroused, empathy vanishes, permanently or temporarily, and the capacity for exploration goes on hold.
>
> — Una McCluskey[31]

A summary provided by Jeremy Lack and Francois Bogacz illustrates the state of parties presenting to an alternative dispute resolution process, with their positions on the conflict and the other party psychologically firmly in place.

> In Positional Dispute Resolution Processes, rather than Interest Based Dispute Resolution processes, the 10 neuro-commandments are likely to be primed negatively due to the inherently competitive or adversarial nature of these processes. The parties will not behave empathetically and will expect to be pressed to make concessions, they will expect and seek to avoid pain, are likely to be dominated by patterns of fear, may have no sense of certainty or predictability due to their perception of the other's irrational or bad-faith behavior and may be influenced by strong emotions of anger. They are likely to avoid all social interaction with the other party (often professing to speak through their lawyers or using caucus meetings if a mediation has been started), and they may feel their sense of status being questioned or undermined. [32]

Example:
Having been accused of wrongful behavior, they may become completely incapable of empathizing with the other side (who is viewed as belonging to an adversarial group), may perceive the other as acting unfairly (thus further exacerbating senses of pain or social exclusion), may feel the other party is impinging on their autonomy, and may be rendered incapable of high order C-system cognitive thinking, as dominant emotional neural networks may consume oxygen and glucose and limit their ability for objective and dispassionate analysis.

Managing the Emotions Expressed by a Party in Mediation

We are hardwired to be alert to the actions or inactions of others that threaten our well-being or interests. When a party is asked a question, the amygdala in their limbic system scans the question to determine whether it is compatible or incompatible with their interests. A question they perceive as threatening engenders a negative emotional reaction. Their brain registers the emotion, and the neural pathways in the brain interpret its meaning, which prompts them to employ behavior that protects their vulnerability.

They may enter an avoid-threat reflex mode. If this happens, their ability to continue to think rationally will depend on the level of emotional stimulation they received, and on their ability to regulate their emotions, which, in turn, depends on their level of emotional intelligence.

Emotions

During mediation sessions, it is essential that a mediator has a heightened sense of emotional awareness so that they notice when a party experiences a negative emotional response. In both private and joint meetings, if a party experiences highly negative emotion, the mediator needs to support them to gently move out of an avoid-threat reflex. This can be done by gradually slowing the pace of the discussion, speaking in a quiet, gentle way, listening attentively to what the party needs to say, and being in the moment with that party.

Affect Labeling

A functional magnetic resonance imaging (MRI) study [33] conducted at the University of California in 2007 showed that affect labeling (using words to describe feelings) produces diminished responses in the amygdala and other limbic regions. Therefore, it is important for parties in conflict to have a space to tell their stories through a process in which they will be heard by the mediator at the first separate private meeting, and by the other party at the joint meeting.

The mediator needs to ask questions in a gentle and empathic way, to support the party to label the emotions they feel. The mediator then needs to slowly and gently reflect back the main points of what the party has said, so that they feel heard and have an opportunity to clarify their thinking. It is only when a party has become calmer that the oxygen and glucose required by the amygdala to process their emotions can shift back to the frontal brain to enable cognitive thinking to take place.

Getting to the Underlying Interests of Parties

Asking questions that translate any threats felt by parties into needs or underlying interests is a way of supporting parties to zone in on the core of their conflict. When a party demonstrates the avoid-threat reflex, identifying what triggered this reflex and its accompanying emotions is the key to getting to the heart of the conflict and to a party's conscious or unconscious concerns, fears and underlying interests.

> All conflicts are perceived by the senses, manifested through body language and kinesthetic sensations, embodied and given meaning by thoughts and ideas, steeped in intense emotions, made conscious through awareness, and may then be resolved by conversations and experiences.
>
> — Kenneth Cloke [34]

The positions adopted and stated by the parties are the gateway to their underlying interests. It is important to note and explore the positions of people in conflict and to use these identified positions, with their accompanying displayed emotions, to get to what lies beneath them. It is by addressing these unseen layers that conflict can be transformed effectively and sustainably.

Chapter 16: Underlying Interests Questions describes the methodology used to get to both the conscious and unconscious underlying interests of parties. Using these methods enables a mediator to support parties to be coherent and congruent about what they wish to say at mediation. In exploring the deeper level of communication between parties, the task of the mediator is to ask questions that will find the unique perspective and paradigm of the parties and the positive intention behind their actions. A mediator's task is to bring the thoughts, assumptions, concerns and fears of the parties from the internal to the external. This should surface any misperceptions, misinterpretations and misunderstandings between parties that may have occurred. These methods are comprehensively covered in Chapter 16.

When underlying interests have been explored and labeled, and when the parties hear and understand the perspective of the other party, it can lead to a paradigm shift in the thinking of both parties, and their approaches to each other. When people have had a chance to talk and vent about their conflict issues, they are ready to hear the other party speak as they will feel less threatened and will be able to think cognitively. This paves the way for an effective and sustainable resolution to be found. A solution that has emanated from merely exploring the positions held by parties may only lead to short-term and topic-specific solutions.

Working with the Brain to Create a Future Without the Problems of the Past

Once parties have understood each other, it is fruitless for a mediator to continue to focus on the past for any longer than is necessary, because this may activate the avoid-threat reflex unnecessarily, lead to amygdala hijack and keep the parties on the treadmill of blame and attack. People find it hard to change their past negative narrative that they have lived within for what may have been years of conflict. This process takes time accompanied by evidential behavioral change. All it takes is for one party to repeat something from the old narrative, such as, "He really should not have done that," to set the other party off with a defensive response. However, it is important to stay in the past long enough to facilitate the parties to vent their feelings and identify their underlying interests and needs.

When no new information or insight is to be gained, asking S4: Future Focus questions from the S Questions Model is a way of changing the negative state and narrative of a party to a more positive narrative with options and possibilities. This will help them to create a future without the problems of the past and will activate their approach-reward reflex. When safety and certainty about the future seem more possible, parties are more open to agreeing on a way forward.

While S4: Future Focus questions are covered comprehensively in Chapter 17, it is important that the value of these questions in mediation be mentioned at this juncture.

Key Learning

- Our brain is biologically hardwired to avoid pain and seek reward. We are more sensitive to danger and fear than to reward.

- Human beings have two basic modes of conscious functioning:
  - The reflexive mode, which is the auto-pilot state of immediate and unconscious reaction that we function in most of the time;
  - The reflective mode, which is the considered and measured response that comes from being emotionally intelligent.

- When a stimulus causes us pain or fear, the first assessment of this is done by the amygdala in the limbic system. If the amygdala is activated, it draws oxygen and glucose away from our frontal brain, which is then left without the necessary resources to perform cognitive thinking.

- When we receive negative social stimuli that leave us feeling under threat, such as during exclusion, bullying or rejection, this activates networks in the brain similar to those activated by physical pain.

- We are programmed to ensure social survival, therefore a threat to any of our SCARF® Drivers of status, certainty, autonomy, relatedness and fairness can engender an emotional reaction and lead to the accompanying avoid-threat reflex.

- A mediator's role is to create a safe and gentle mediation process where conflicting parties can have the real conversation they were unable to have on their own, because either they were in default mode and could not verbalize their thoughts clearly; they were afraid to verbalize their thoughts to the other person; or they did not have a formal opportunity to engage with the other party.

- Listening skills and questioning tools need to be used to facilitate a party in mediation to cope with an avoid-threat reflex, but only after a party has had an opportunity to express their emotions safely and effectively.

- During mediation, it is counterproductive to focus on the past any longer than is necessary as this may reignite the conflict. However, it is important to stay in the past long enough to facilitate the parties to identify their underlying interests and needs.

- A mediator needs to switch to asking S4: Future Focus questions once underlying interests have been identified, parties have heard and understood each other and there is no new information or insight to be gained.

- Section 4 has comprehensive information on developing questions in line with the theories in this chapter.

Section 2

Practical Application of the S Questions Model

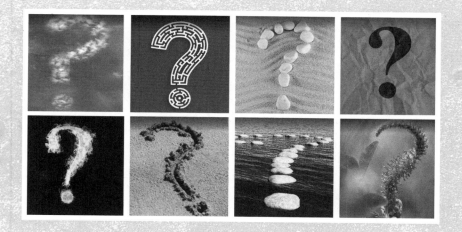

Methodology to Minimize an Avoid-threat Reflex When Asking Questions

Methodology

Tʜɪs ᴄʜᴀᴘᴛᴇʀ ᴄᴏᴠᴇʀs ᴛʜᴇ ᴍᴇᴛʜᴏᴅᴏʟᴏɢʏ and approach that need to be employed when asking questions so that an avoid-threat reflex response to any stimulus will not be inadvertently experienced by the parties and result in them experiencing an unnecessary amygdala hijack.

This methodology is outlined under three headings:

1. Mediation Framework
2. Mediator's Approach
3. Mediation Skills and Techniques

As well as the general guidelines for asking questions outlined in this chapter, there are also additional and specific guidelines for asking some of the questions from the S4: Shift Thinking Dimension of questions, namely: S4: Journey of Inference questions, S4: Cognitive Elements questions, and S4: Underlying Interests questions. There additional guidelines are outlined in the sections covering these questions.

1. Mediation Framework

As stated in the introduction to this book, the S Questions Model is designed on the premise that an initial separate and private meeting will take place with each of the parties prior to bringing them together for a joint meeting, and that separate meetings are part of the structure of the joint meeting, if necessary, and appropriate to the needs of the process and the parties.

Hold Separate Private Meetings

Parties in conflict need to build trust with their mediator prior to being in a room with the other party. Holding an initial separate meeting creates a space for this to happen. To do otherwise heightens the level of threat that parties coming to a joint meeting may feel, and this could be aggravated by a mediator who, because they are working in a vacuum of knowledge about the parties, could inadvertently ask questions that could stimulate an unnecessary avoid-threat reflex in the parties.

This initial separate meeting creates a forum where discussion can take place about issues that may be sensitive for a party and that could result in them becoming vulnerable in front of the other party. Some of the deeper and more searching questions that are contained in the S4: Shift Thinking Dimension of questions need to be initially asked at this separate meeting to judge the appropriateness of asking them at the joint meeting. It is important that a party is not inadvertently asked a question at a joint meeting that may result in them losing face or becoming vulnerable or feeling threatened.

2. Mediator's Approach

> There are two fundamental things people are asking for in any relationship: "Do I matter?" and "Am I heard?"
>
> — Jane Gunn, Corporate Peacemakers

Body Language

The meaning and intention behind what a mediator says is conveyed through their body language, their tone of voice and the words that they verbalize. These three elements need to be congruent with each other. If not, the receiver of the message will be more influenced by what is conveyed through the nonverbal body language used than by the words used. If the body language is threatening or judgmental, then this negativity is what will be understood. Parties will not feel that they matter and are heard.

Albert Mehrabian, Professor Emeritus of Psychology, UCLA, has become best known for his publications on the relative percentage importance of verbal and nonverbal messages. Mehrabian's theory is that the type of body language and tone of voice used by a person conveys the intention of their message more than the actual words they use.

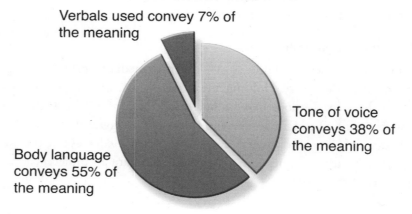

The Message Conveyed

Verbals used convey 7% of the meaning

Tone of voice conveys 38% of the meaning

Body language conveys 55% of the meaning

Figure 4.1.

CREDIT: O'SULLIVAN SOLUTIONS

EFFECTIVE BODY LANGUAGE

When a mediator is listening to parties and asking questions, the body language they display needs to convey respect and impartiality or multi-partiality, accompanied by an open body language stance and gentle eye contact. Forming eye contact does not mean staring eyeball to eyeball but looking at the general triangle formed by the eyebrows and the mouth. Mediators need to imagine themselves as a blank sheet of paper waiting to be filled with information from the parties, and even a bit like the TV character detective Colombo, who asked his questions in an apparent charming, innocent manner. His body language was reflective, tentative, gentle and curious.

Use the Principles of Mediation as a Reference Point Before Asking a Question

When in doubt as to whether to ask a particular question, one of the things that may help is to use the principles of mediation as a reference point. If the type of question, or the stage at which a mediator would like to ask it, contravenes any of these mediation principles, then caution is urged.

Principles of Mediation (VICS):
- Voluntariness
- Impartiality / Multi-partiality
- Confidentiality
- Self-determination

Be Curious

Try to figure out the things that the one party would like to know about the other party, and, if it is appropriate, ask these questions in a curious, gentle and caring way.

Create Opportunities for the Empowerment of Parties

Mediators need to believe in a party's capacity to know the right answers, as they are the experts of their own conflict. But on appropriate occasions during a mediation process, and when a mediator deems that the climate is conducive to it, parties can also be asked what questions they think are necessary to ask of themselves and of the other party.

Use SCARF® Drivers Questions to Facilitate Empowerment of the Parties

Social Driver	Mediator's Empowering Question	Mediator's Intention
Status	If I was to ask you just one question, what would that be?	To recognize the party as the expert on their own life.
Certainty	What question, if asked, could make the most difference to your future?	To allow the parties some control of their own futures.
Autonomy	What are the questions that I need to ask you so that your problem with each other will be solved?	To respect the parties' capacity to solve their own problem.
Relatedness	What questions do I need to ask you that will help each of you to be understood by the other?	To give the responsibility for connectedness to both parties.
Fairness	What question(s) need to be asked to enable you to solve this issue in a way that is fair to both of you? How might this option meet the interests and needs of both of you?	To ask each of the parties to jointly work out what is fair for both of them.

3. Mediation Skills and Techniques

Use Signposting Prior to Asking a Question

Parties coming to mediation for the first time may be worried about the process and procedures that will be used. Letting them know *what* is going to be done, and *how* it is going to be done, will lessen their anxiety. This is called signposting, and doing it will reduce any feelings of threat the parties may have.

> Example:
>
> - First, I will start with Karen, and I will give her all the time she needs to speak, then I will ask you the same question, Tom, and I will also give you whatever time you need to speak, then I will ask you both....
> - Tom, I need to stay with Karen for just a little time more, and then I will give you plenty of time to say all that you need to say....

Ask Permission Prior to Asking a Difficult Question

Sometimes it may be appropriate to ask a party for permission before asking a difficult or sensitive question. This needs to be signposted.

> Example:
>
> This may seem like a difficult question, and I am not sure how you might feel about responding to it? May I please have your permission to ask it, and then you can decide whether you wish to respond?

Intermittently, and When Appropriate, Reflect Back What You Have Heard from a Party Prior to Asking a Question

Repeatedly asking questions may become intimidating for the parties, so it is important to intersperse questions with reflections on what you have heard, so that the parties do not feel as if they are being interrogated by question after question:

> Example:
>
> Tom, I hear you saying that you were quite shocked when that happened; what was the worst thing for you?

Capture the Gems from the Parties' Communication

When parties feel threatened, they may only hear the negative things that are said by the other party and may miss positive or helpful comments, which I refer to as *gems*. It is the role of the mediator to catch these gems and bring them into the discussion at a time that is appropriate. A gem is a piece of information that one party gives that could be valuable to the creating of understanding between the parties.

Examples of gems:

- When parties express similar feelings, even if they are negative, they need to be captured and used appropriately later: So, you were both very worried?
- When a party expresses a regret or apology. This is important, as the other party will then understand that the other gets it, and the mediator can then explore what the party could do differently if they could go back and address the past conflict with their current information.
- If one party says something positive about the other, a mediator needs to clearly reflect back this statement so that the other party hears it.
- If a party voices hope or possibility for the future as this demonstrates a belief in a different future.
- When a party talks about the impact the conflict has on them, this can be explored in more detail and may identify the party's underlying interests.
- If one party expresses recognition of the impact on the other party, this needs to be reflected back by the mediator so that the other party hears it.
- When a party concludes the telling of their story and experience, the last sentence or words stated by them are often their conclusion about what they have just voiced. It is important to capture this gem as it may be a key to their underlying interests or their hopes.
- If a party identifies a possible solution, then perhaps a small agreement could be made at that stage, or it could be introduced at a later stage.

Example:

Mediator: Tom, I heard you mention earlier that you wished that Karen had come directly to you

- If Karen had done that, how would it have been for you?
- What would have been your response to Karen?
- What would have been the outcome?

Karen, if that had happened, how might it have been for you?

Mutualize and Create Relatedness Prior to Asking Questions

When parties express feelings that are similar, such as wishes, feelings, experiences or difficulties, it is vital to pick up on this and to repeat these feelings back to them as a preface for asking a question. This has a strong impact on the dynamic at play in mediation.

> Example:
>
> I hear you both saying that your sleep has been seriously disrupted since this conflict started.

> Example:
>
> I have heard you *both* mention that the dynamic between you has changed, and you have *both* said that you would prefer that it was not this way. What way would you *each* like it to be in the future? I will ask Tom first, and then I will ask you, Karen.

When parties in mediation shift from blaming each other, to the place where they realize that they *both* have a problem that they *both* need to solve, then finding a solution to the conflict becomes more achievable. Facilitating parties to identify similarities and common problems, and then mutualizing these prior to asking a question, results in their sense of relatedness increasing.

> Example:
>
> For *both of you* this has been a particularly difficult time, and for *both of you* the impact has been huge; may I please ask you *both* a question about this?

Move from a Past and Negative Narrative into a Future and Positive Narrative

The focus and thinking of parties in mediation is influenced and driven by the kind of questions they are asked. The quality and strategic focus of the question will influence the connections generated in the brain, and this will affect the quality of their thinking and, ultimately, the quality of their responses. Moving parties from a past narrative to a future narrative should only be done after parties have had an opportunity to express their emotions.

Example:

If you ask a question that is problem focused, you may get responses about the problem accompanied by negative emotions regarding the past. But if you ask an effective S4: Future Focus question, then the response will include the opportunities and possibilities for the future, with accompanying hopeful and positive emotions. To do this, the party is asked to consider a world in which the problem has been solved. (Future Focus questions are described in detailed in Chapter 17.)

Example:

Party says: She should stop behaving like that! (Old narrative)

Mediator's reframe: How would you like Karen to be from now on? (Moving to a new narrative)

Example:

Party says: It would never work. (Old narrative)

Mediator asks: What would it be like if it did work? (Moving to a new narrative)

If it did work, what would have happened that would have resulted in it working? (Moving to a new narrative)

Use Impartial and Neutral Questions

Questions need to be asked in a neutral way so that the mediator is not perceived by either of the parties as being biased toward the other party.

TRANSLATE A QUESTION THAT MAY BE PERCEIVED AS PARTIAL INTO A "BOTH" QUESTION

When asking a question that might be perceived as judgmental, signpost it and ask it of both parties, if appropriate.

> Example:
>
> I would like to ask *both of you* a question, I will ask you first, Tom, and then I will ask you, Karen…. In what way might the thinking of *each of you* be blocking resolution?

INTRODUCE REPORTING VERBS INTO THE QUESTION

When reflecting back to a party what they have said, and before asking them a question, ensure that the words being reflected back do not give the impression that the views expressed are anything other than the party's words and are not the mediator's words. This is done by introducing reporting verbs into what you reflect back.

> Example:
>
> Instead of reflecting back to the party —
>
> You are feeling isolated and no one will talk to you at work and Tom should do something about this?
>
> Replace it with:
>
> You are *saying* that you feel isolated and you also *add* that no one talks to you at work, and you *mentioned* that you would like Tom to do something about this…. What would you need from Tom for this to be resolved in an acceptable way?

REMOVE BLAME BY USING PASSIVE VOICE INSTEAD OF ACTIVE VOICE

Reflecting back to a party what they said, in an impartial way, before you ask a question, removes the element of blame from a party. This is done by not referring to the party who carried out the action by their name (removing the subject) and changing the question construction from active voice to passive voice.

Active Voice	Passive Voice
"He levelled the boundary wall." This sentence identifies who did the action.	"The boundary wall was levelled." In this reframed sentence, the person who carried out the action is not named.
"She puts pressure on me." This sentence identifies who is to blame.	"You feel pressured?" This reframed sentence is changed from active to passive voice, and the focus is on the impact on the person rather than on who is to blame.

REMAIN NONDIRECTIVE WHEN EXPLORING POSSIBILITIES

To remain nondirective when asking a question, avoid using words such as *should* or *must*. By remaining nondirective, the party is asked to consider what the other party could or might need rather than being told to make a commitment. This lessens any threat that a party may feel.

Example:

Instead of asking, what *should* you give Tom?

Ask instead, what *could* you offer to Tom?

Instead of asking, what *must* you offer to Tom?

Ask instead, what *might* Tom need?

MANAGE QUESTIONS WITHOUT ENGENDERING POWERLESSNESS IN A PARTY

Asking a party how an event or a person "made them feel" may convey to that party that they have no control over their emotions, and that the other party is completely responsible for their emotional response.

Example:

Instead of saying to the party:

How did that make you feel? (Active voice)

Replace it with more neutral language:

What was that like for you? (Passive voice)

How did that impact on you? (Passive voice)

Reframe Toxic Statements Prior to Posing a Question

Reframing is the art of restating any toxic expressions used by a party in a less threatening manner, without compromising the truth of the statement. The other party will then hear what was said in a manner that seems less threatening.

Note the toxic expressions used by parties during the separate private meeting. Reframe these toxic expressions before asking a question, but not at the expense of the truth. Instead, reframe them in a way that focuses on the possible impacts they may have on the party.

Example:

Karen says: He bullies me to get it done on time!

Mediator's reframe: I hear you saying that you feel pressured to get things done on time; what is this like for you?

or

Ask the party how they would have liked it to have been different, or how they would like it to be in the future.

Example:

Karen says: He bullies me to get it done on time!

Mediator's reframe: I hear you saying that you feel pressured to get things done on time; how would you have liked it to have been different?

or

How would you like Tom to be different in the future?

USE THE NAME OF THE PARTY

Always use the name of a party to whom you are referring. If a party refers to another party by saying he or she, the mediator needs to ensure that they themselves use the name of that other party in any communication during mediation.

REPLACE WORDS SUCH AS *BUT* AND *HOWEVER* WITH A WORD LIKE *AND*

When two points are being made in a sentence, and if they are linked with words like *but* or *however*, it breaks the sentence in two and creates an opposition between the two points being made:

She was good at the start; however, her standards have dropped.

Additionally, it can make one part conditional on the other part:

I will do it, but only if she…

Using the word *and* joins the two statements without creating a stark opposition. While the two parts of the sentence are still perceived as being less closely related to each other, their opposition to each other is not as stark.

In the example here, the reframe used by the mediator shows that Tom is willing to do something and it would be helpful if Karen did the other. This will be less grating for Karen to hear.

Example:

Tom says: I would do that *but* not until she does the other!

Mediator's reframe: You are saying that you are willing to do that *and* it would be helpful if Karen did the other?

AVOID REFLECTING BACK STRONGLY NEGATIVE ADJECTIVES

Instead of repeating a strong negative adjective used by a party, either ask for specific examples, or ask about the impact, or focus on the feelings of the party using the negative adjective:

Example:

Tom says:

> She might have been good at the start, but now she is *useless* at managing the project's budget!

Mediator's reframe before asking a question:

> Tom, it sounds like you are saying that Karen was good at the start *and* you are concerned at the way in which she manages the budget; **can you be a little more specific about your concerns?**

> or

> Tom, it sounds like you are saying that Karen was good at the start and you are now concerned at the way in which she manages the budget; **how is this impacting on the organization?**

> or

> Tom, it sounds like you are saying that Karen was good at the start and you are concerned at the way in which she manages the budget; **what is this like for you?**

SEPARATE THE DEED FROM THE DOER

Focus on the deed done rather than on the person who did it and ask for an example.

> Example:
>
> Replace the doer (he) when a party exclaims:
>
> He is a liar!
>
> With the deed:
>
> Have you an example of when you felt you were not told the truth by Tom?

Be Aware of the Concept of Risk (Loss) Aversion When Posing a Question

Studies on negotiation have established that parties make different decisions about risk, depending upon whether they view that risk as a possible gain or a possible loss. This, in turn, will determine whether they experience an approach-reward reflex or a an avoid-threat reflex. If a party *loses* ten dollars they register a higher level of threat response than the level of reward response they register if they *find* ten dollars.

> Example:
>
> If a party is looking for a settlement figure of $100,000 and the other side is offering $75,000, then the party will react more positively to a question that is phrased as a gain, rather than to a loss, even though the numerical value is the same:
>
> An offer perceived as a **gain:**
>
> > You have a definite offer of $75,000 which is a certain payment… how might you respond to this offer?
>
> An offer perceived as a **loss:**
>
> > You have an offer that is $25,000 less than you had hoped to receive… how might you respond to this offer?

A mediator needs to know the effect of any question that focuses on loss, as opposed to gain, so that when a party seems to only focus on what they may lose compared to what they may gain, the mediator will be able to address this with some comparative and reality-testing questions so that the feeling of threat is minimized for that party.

> Example:
>
> In broad terms, what will this give you, that you do not have already?

Use NLP Representational Systems When Asking Questions

Richard Bandler and John Grinder, the cofounders of NLP, state that we absorb information and represent it to our brain through the channels of our five senses. These channels are known as representational systems. As noted in Chapter 2: How We Process and Communicate Information, these channels that absorb information are visual (images), auditory (sounds), kinesthetic (touch and internal feelings) and, to a lesser extent, gustatory (tastes) and olfactory (smells).

Bandler and Grinder claim that each person has a more highly valued or preferred representational system in which they vividly create an experience in their brain; and each person tends to use that specific representational system in their communication more often than their other representational systems.

When mediators listen to the surface level of language and communication that presents at mediation, they need to note the representational system parties use when communicating their experience. Then mediators need to use that same representational language when reflecting back what parties say, prior to asking questions of them.

For communication between parties to be effective, mediators need to be certain that a party hears a message as it was intended by the sender, the other party. If one party is using visual references and the other party is auditory, they may have mismatched communications. A mediator needs to reflect back to the party who uses this representational system using visual references, and then ask a question of the other party using the auditory representational system.

Party's Preferred Representational Sense	A Mediator Needs to Use Representational Systems to Communicate Effectively and Build Rapport
Visual	I can **see** you are delighted with the project, how do you think other people are **viewing** it?
Auditory	It **sounds** to me like you are pleased with the project. What are the things you have been **hearing** about it?
Kinesthetic	I **sense** that you **feel** a very **heavy burden** on you since this happened. What would help you in **lifting** that **heavy burden**? What sort of **supports** from the organization do you **feel** may **lighten** this burden?
Olfactory	You say there is a **smell** of something fishy about this project; what exactly is that **smell** telling you?
Gustatory	You say that you can **taste** the victory; what do you most **relish** about it?

Key Learning

This checklist identifies the key methodologies that need to be used for asking questions, to lessen the chances of an avoid-threat reflex response in a party.

SUMMARY CHECKLIST OF METHODOLOGIES FOR ASKING QUESTIONS IN MEDIATION

Mediation Framework

✓ There is a need to hold initial separate and private meetings with the parties, and also to incorporate the holding of separate and private meetings during the joint meeting, as appropriate.

Mediator's Approach

✓ Use body language that displays neutrality, nonjudgment, gentleness, sincere interest and innocent curiosity.

✓ When in doubt as to whether to ask a particular question, one of the things that may help is to use the principles of mediation as a reference point.

✓ Create opportunities to empower both parties.

Skills and Techniques

✓ Use signposting prior to asking a question

✓ Ask permission prior to asking a difficult question

✓ At times, reflect back what you have heard from a party, prior to asking a question

✓ Capture and use the "gems" from the parties' communication

✓ Mutualize and create relatedness, by using words like *both* and *each of you* prior to asking questions

✓ Move from a past and negative narrative into a future and positive narrative

✓ Use impartial and neutral questions:

- Translate a question that may be perceived as judgmental into a *both* question
- Introduce "reporting verbs" into a question
- Remove blame when developing questions by using a passive voice rather than an active voice
- Remain nondirective when exploring possibilities
- Manage questions without generating powerlessness in a party

✓ Reframe toxic statements prior to posing a question:

- Replace any toxic words used by a party, but retain the truth, when reflecting back what a party has said
- When referring to a party, use their name rather than *he* or *she*
- Replace *but* and *however* with *and*
- Avoid reflecting back strongly negative adjectives that one party may use about the other party, and either ask for specific examples or ask about the impact, or focus on the feelings of the party using the negative adjective
- Separate the deed from the doer

✓ Be aware of the concept of risk (loss) aversion when posing a question

✓ Use NLP-based representational systems when asking questions

The S Questions Model Applied to a Mediation Process

Reflective Preparation for Questions

WHEN PREPARING FOR MEDIATION, or during a mediation process, a mediator needs to ensure that the questions they develop are strategic, relevant and appropriate.

They need to be able to anticipate, as much as possible, the kind of responses that people may have when asked specific types of questions in case a question inadvertently triggers an amygdala hijack. It is always wise to first try out any sensitive question in a separate private meeting before asking it at a joint meeting, so that parties do not feel threatened, vulnerable or unsafe at a joint meeting.

A mediator can prepare by reflecting on some questions...

✓ What might I need to ask questions about?

✓ What might parties need to ask each other about?

✓ What might I need to know? What might parties need to know?

✓ What might I know already? What might parties know already?

✓ What might I not know? What might parties not know?

✓ What might I *think* I know, and where is my evidence for this? What do parties *think* they know, and what might be their evidence for this?

✓ How will I find out what I might not know?

✓ Is there a question that is not obvious to me?

✓ What do I want each of these questions to do or to achieve?

✓ Is there another question or a deeper question that I could ask?

✓ At what forum should I ask any of these questions: initial separate meetings, joint meeting or at separate meetings during the joint meeting?

The S Questions Model

Chapter 1 gave an overview of the S Questions Model. This chapter gives comprehensive information on how to use the model and on the purpose, development and application of each of the S1, S2, S3 and S4 dimensions of it. To recap, the model was developed to incorporate an extensive range of questions that can be asked in a mediation process into one clear and accessible image.

The Four Dimensions of Questions in the S Questions Model

There are four dimensions of questions in the S Questions Model and these are categorized and labeled as follows:

- S1: Subject Matter Dimension of questions
- S2: Structure Dimension of questions
- S3: Seeking Information Dimension of questions
- S4: Shift Thinking Dimension of questions

S1: Subject Matter Dimension of Questions

All questions incorporate the S1: Subject Matter Dimension of questions and can be asked about the people involved in the conflict; the environment or context in which the conflict takes place; the problem or issue presented to mediation; and the interaction of the people, the environment and the problem.

S2: Structure Dimension of Questions

All questions have an S2: Structure Dimension of questions incorporated in them, in that an open or closed question may be chosen. After first deciding the subject matter and the structure of a question, the choice is then between asking an S3 or an S4 question, or a combination of both.

S3: Seeking Information Dimension of Questions

These are simple, linear questions that clarify existing information or introduce information that is either previously known, or is not already known, by each of the parties. An S3 question strategically targets the information that is required from the parties for the conversations that take place during a mediation process.

S4: Shift Thinking Dimension of Questions

These questions are designed to uncover information that specifically creates new insight for the parties. The intention is to shift their thinking so that they experience a paradigm shift and look at the other party and their conflict in a different light.

While there are eight S4 questions and they are presented in the model in a certain order, each one is a stand-alone question with its own unique purpose. Each S4 category of questions may also be linked with each of the other seven categories to achieve a specific outcome. In general, the S4 questions move from hearing what happened and how a party interpreted it and acted upon it, to distilling and exploring the information presented, to making connections with other experiences or events. The questions help to identify any inner conflict or inconsistencies within a party, to safely teasing out alternative perspectives. They identify the core of a problem and facilitate the creation of a future without the problems of the past.

The S Questions Model

S1 Subject Matter Dimension of Questions
Encompass the subject matter that is being discussed

People
The parties' internal and external narratives, with their underlying interests and positions

Environment
The environment in which the parties are operating (physical, social and psychological)

Problem
That which is presenting at mediation

PEP interaction
How the People, the Environment and the Problem interact, influence and impact on each other

S2 Structure Dimension of Questions

The construction of a question can be phrased as an open question or a closed question.

Closed questions require a yes or no response.

Open questions are introduced with - Who? When? Where? Which? What? How? In what way? What if? If...?

Rarely use *Why* as it may be judgmental and result in the party needing to justify their actions.

S3 Seeking Information Dimension of Questions
Information gathering questions about S1: Subject Matter Dimension of Questions, incorporating the People, Environment, and Problem (PEP) and PEP interaction

These questions clarify information given by parties and invite the parties' perspective on the conflict. They are a statement from the party's already held beliefs and opinions and form the pool of information about the conflict from which S4: Shift Thinking Dimension of Questions can be explored.

S4 Shift Thinking Dimension of Questions
To uncover new information and insight, either by exploring and focusing thinking or by connecting and expanding thinking, leading to a paradigm shift

Journey of Inference Questions
Interpretations, Assumptions, Conclusions, Beliefs, Actions
Purpose: To identify the link between interpretations and actions. To explore parties' current narratives and to shift perspectives toward a new narrative.

Neuro-linguistic Programming (NLP) Based Questions
Deletions, Distortions, Generalizations
Purpose: To bring clarity, explore subjective realities, explore bias and misinterpretations, and create congruency in communication.

Distinctions and Differences Questions
People, Parts, Contexts, Opposites, Spatial, Comparisons, Time Span, Measurement or Ranking
Purpose: To bring clarity, relevance, measurement, boundary and a different perspective to the conflict.

Reflective Connecting Questions
Connecting with patterns and cycles of conflict, both intrapersonal and interpersonal, and in the broader context
Purpose: To raise awareness of negative patterns and cycles of conflict, to deconstruct past unhelpful patterns and to reconstruct new healthy patterns

Cognitive Elements-based Questions
Knowledge; Opinion and Thinking; Beliefs, Values and Attitudes; Behaviour; Sense of Self/Identity; Environment
Purpose: To explore inner conflicts and inconsistencies between perception and reality, and between the six cognitive elements. To seek a paradigm shift that will restore cognitive consonance.

Other People Questions
Explore an imagined perspective of the other party, a third party, a cultural norm or hypothetical parties
Purpose: To open perspectives and create insight, safely.

Underlying Interests Questions
Conflict Triggers, Impact, Beliefs, Values and Attitudes
Purpose: To move from the conflict positions of the parties to the core of their conflict, and identify needs and underlying interests.

Future Focus Questions
Hypothetical, Conditional, Consequential, BATNA / MLATNA / WATNA
Purpose: To move parties off the conflict treadmill and facilitate cognitive thinking, leading to options and solutions.

Figure: 5.1.

© www.osullivansolutions.ie

S Questions Model Applied to Initial Separate Meeting

S Questions Model	Question Tasks	Mediator's Reflections
S1 Subject Matter questions People, Environment, Problem, PEP Interaction	**To identify the subject matter for discussion**	Clarity about issues
S2 Structure questions Open/Closed questions	**Extent of the information required** Closed questions for yes/no response Open questions for elaboration	Information needed for discussions
S3 Seeking Information questions Information gathering/clarification	**To seek and clarify information** Storytelling: Hear parties' story Identify and explore issues and positions Prioritise and categorise issues	**Reflection prior to Joint Session** Categories of issues? The priorities? Any misunderstandings?
	Mediator's internal reassessment of: Conflict Analysis map Range of Hypothesis Any supports/professional advice needed?	**Adjustments** Conflict Analysis map? Hypothesis amendment? Supports/professional advice needed?
S4 Shift Thinking questions Journey of Inference NLP based Cognitive Elements-based Distinction and Difference Reflecting Connecting Other People Underlying Interests	**To identify and explore:** Information gaps/misinformation Perceptions, thinking and attitudes Interpretations and assumptions Behaviour Any Journeys of Inference? Any cognitive dissonance presenting?	**Reflection prior to Joint Session** Information deletion, distortion, generalization? Journeys of Inference? Misunderstanding and misperceptions? Cognitive dissonance? Underlying interests?

To gain understanding
Uncover underlying interests: conscious and unconscious*

Conscious *Generic questions*	**Unconscious** *Additional questions*
Conflict positions?	Conflict Triggers?
Impact?	Emotional responses to
Emotions?	conflict trigger?
Concerns/Worries?	'SCARF® Drivers'
Needs?	Values/Beliefs/Attitudes?

To check understanding and orientation of parties
Parties' capacity to self-reflect and understand each other?
Parties' orientation towards problem solving and agreement?
Parties' potential solutions?

*Private meetings can be used to test the safety of asking some questions.

Reflection prior to Joint Session
Parties' capacity to self-reflect and understand each other?
Parties' orientation towards problem solving and agreement?
Possible solutions from Parties?
Vulnerability of parties if using S4 questions?
Opportunities for mutualizing
Toxic language reframing?

Figure: 5.2.

S Questions Model Applied to Joint Meeting

S Questions Model	Question Tasks	Questions Outcome
S1 Subject Matter questions People, Environment, Problem, PEP Interaction	**To identify the subject matter for discussion**	Information and clarity
S2 Structure questions Open/Closed questions	**Extent of the information required** Closed questions for yes/no response Open questions for elaboration	Information and clarity to inform agenda and discussions
S3 Seeking Information questions Information gathering/clarification	**To gather and clarify information:** To check understanding of the mediation process To explore ground rules To facilitate parties to tell their stories To introduce new information and clarify existing information	Existing information clarified New information uncovered
S4 Shift Thinking questions Journey of Inference NLP Distinction and Difference Reflecting Connecting Cognitive Elements Other People Underlying Interests Future Focus	**To check parties':** Information gaps/misinformation Perceptions, thinking and attitudes Interpretations and assumptions Behaviour Any Journeys of Inference made? Any cognitive dissonance?	**Understanding created by:** Exploring and focusing thinking Broadening and expanding thinking leading to the creation of a Paradigm Shift
	To create understanding between the parties Uncover underlying interests: conscious and unconscious*	**Understanding created by:** Identifying and exploring Underlying Interests leading to the creation of a Paradigm Shift
	Conscious **Unconscious** *Generic questions* *Additional questions* Conflict positions? Conflict triggers? Impact? Emotional responses to Emotions? conflict trigger? Concerns/Worries? 'SCARF® Drivers' Needs? Values/Beliefs/Attitudes?	
	To move towards the future Options development Reality test options Choose options Agreements reached	**Mediated agreement:** A future identified, without the problems of the past Agreement written and signed
	*Private meetings can be used to test the safety of asking some questions.	

Figure: 5.3.

Section 3

Practical Application of S1, S2 and S3 Questions

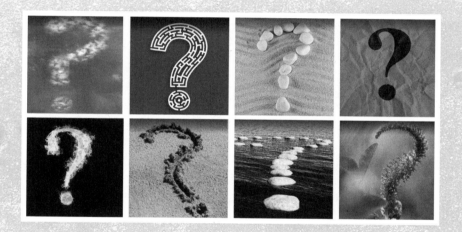

S1: The Subject Matter Dimension of Questions

Asking questions to seek information and clarification about S1: Subject Matter Dimension of Questions:

People - the parties' internal and external narratives, with their underlying interests and positions.

Environment - the environment in which the parties are operating (physical, social and psychological)

Problem - that which is presenting at mediation

PEP interaction - how the People, the Environment and the Problem interact, influence and impact on each other

© www.osullivansolutions.ie

THE PURPOSE OF THE S1: SUBJECT MATTER DIMENSION OF QUESTIONS is to introduce all the information that is pertinent to the mediation agenda regarding:

Figure: 6.1.

CREDIT: O'SULLIVAN SOLUTIONS

- The people involved in the conflict
- The environment (physical, social and psychological) in which the conflict takes place
- The problem that is the subject matter of the conflict
- The PEP interaction — the interaction of the people, the environment and the problem

S1: Subject Matter Dimension of Questions: People, Environment, Problem, PEP Interaction

People

S1 questions need to identify and explore any information about the parties that is relevant to the mediation process.

THE NEEDS OF THE PARTIES FROM THE MEDIATION PROCESS

✓ What do parties need from the mediation process, the mediator and the other party?

✓ What outcomes do the parties require?

✓ What are the things that one party would like to know from the other party?

THE PARADIGM OF THE PARTIES

✓ What positions do the parties adopt?

✓ How do the parties justify and defend their positions?

✓ What is the unique perspective or paradigm of the parties?

✓ What are the meanings, assumptions and conclusions that parties reached about the conflict, and how that feeds into their beliefs and actions?

✓ Are there any misunderstandings or differences in perspectives between the parties regarding the problem?

✓ Is there any cognitive dissonance within either or both parties?

✓ How do the parties communicate with and relate to each other, before or during the conflict?

THE UNDERLYING INTERESTS OF THE PARTIES

✓ How are parties experiencing the conflict; what approach have they taken to it and what challenges are they facing?

✓ What was the conflict trigger for each of the parties? What did this engender within the parties?

✓ How have the domains of the SCARF® Drivers Model (status, certainty, autonomy, relatedness and fairness) been impacted?

✓ What are the other impacts from the conflict on the parties, their emotions, concerns and worries?

✓ What are the beliefs and values of the parties and what is important to them?

✓ What are the conscious and unconscious underlying interests of the parties that need to be met?

Hazard Warning

If a mediator is unsure whether asking a question at a joint meeting may result in a party feeling inadvertently threatened or vulnerable in front of the other party, then the question needs to be checked at a separate private meeting first.

OPTIONS FOR SOLUTIONS

✓ What is the price people are paying for this conflict?

✓ What is the payoff parties may be getting from the conflict, and which they may be slow to relinquish?

✓ Are there any cognitive dissonance blocks to resolution, or any other blocks?

✓ What are the options for movement toward agreements that meet the underlying interests and needs of the parties?

Environment

These questions include the social, psychological and physical environment in which the parties are situated. They apply to all mediation sectors.

✓ Geographical or physical factors?

✓ Structures in the environment/organization?

✓ Roles and responsibilities of parties in the environment/organization?

✓ Communication systems — the accepted formal/nonformal systems in the environment/organization?

✓ How information is disseminated?

✓ The decision-making process used in the environment? Consultation processes?

✓ Ownership and distribution of resources in the environment?

✓ The conflict dynamic, and how conflict is managed in the environment?

✓ Culture — boundaries and norms of the environment?

✓ The values underpinning the culture?

✓ Previous attempts at conflict solution?

Problem

These questions need to explore and identify any information about the problem that is relevant to the mediation process.

✓ The problem and the issues presenting?

✓ The nature of the problem: structural, communication, relationship, value-based, interest-based?

✓ The scope of the problem?

✓ The causes of the problem? The causes of the causes of the problem? The causes of the causes of the causes of the problem?

✓ The impact of the conflict on the ongoing problem?

✓ The interior and exterior blocks to possible solutions?

✓ The possible options for solution that might solve the problem?

PEP Interaction

These questions explore and identify any issues regarding the interaction of the people, the environment and the problem.

✓ How the people, the environment and the problem (PEP) interact, influence and impact on each other, particularly with regard to the cause of the conflict, its continuation or escalation?

✓ The connections between the context of the dispute, the people involved, the emotions of the parties, their past and current history in relation to each other and to their views about each other?

✓ The impact of the behaviors of people on the problem, the culture, the dynamic and the atmosphere in the environment?

✓ The impact of the problem, or the culture, or the dynamic or the atmosphere in the environment on the people involved in the conflict?

✓ The external influences on the people and the problem that contribute to the impact and escalation of the problem?

S2: The Structure Dimension of Questions

The construction of a question can be phrased as an open question or a closed question.	**Closed** questions require a yes or no response. **Open** questions are introduced with - Who? When? Where? Which? What? How? In what way? What if? If...?	**Rarely** use *Why* as it may be judgmental and result in the party needing to justify their actions.

© www.osullivansolutions.ie

THE S2: STRUCTURE QUESTIONS incorporate the ways in which a question can be structured: either as a closed question or as an open question. Ask a closed question if you are looking for a Yes or a No response with no additional information needed. It is a direct question; it is to the point, and it does not encourage elaboration. Alternatively, the purpose of an open question is to encourage elaboration in the response and the introduction of additional and broader information.

Figure: 7.1.

CREDIT: O'SULLIVAN SOLUTIONS

Closed Questions

If the mediator requires only a Yes or No answer without any additional information, a closed question is appropriate. A problem arises when more information is required and it is sought by mistakenly asking a closed question. However, there are situations when you specifically need a Yes or a No response and when asking a closed question is appropriate.

Examples of appropriate closed questions:

- Are you both ready to start the mediation process now?
- Have you received advice from your legal and financial advisers about this?
- Am I hearing you saying that...?
- Are you both in agreement that this is the next topic for discussion?

Examples of inappropriate closed questions that will curtail the amount of information and even invite resistance:

- Was it your approach that caused this outcome?
- Would it not have been better if you had not said that?
- Was there not a better way you could have done this?

When used inappropriately, closed questions can be perceived as leading, directive or judgmental, as they often emanate from the mediator's own thoughts, assumptions, opinions, beliefs and values. They often serve the agenda of the questioner and can lead to a party feeling entrapped.

Open Questions

Open questions start with Who, When, Where, Which, What, How, In what way, If or What if? This image illustrates the hierarchy of open questions. The more powerful questions are at the top of the steps and will stimulate more reflective thinking.

Figure: 7.2.

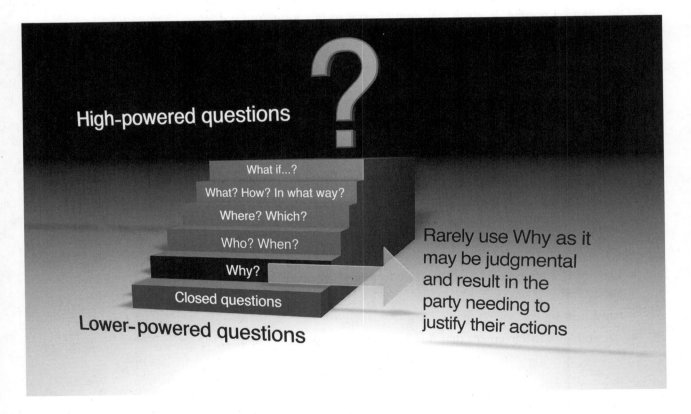

The Hierarchy of Open Questions — Less Powerful to More Powerful

Who

- Who has challenged you around this?
- Who has been impacted the most by this?
- Who could support you with this issue you describe?

When

- When did that first occur?
- When did the other events take place?
- When did you first know that there was tension?

Where

- Where were you when you heard that?
- Where does this mostly happen?
- Where could each of you start to make a change?

Which

- In which context is this worse?
- Which of those incidents impacted on you the most?
- With which member do you have most difficulty?

What

- What was it that concerned you the most?
- What did you think this meant?
- What could each of you have done differently so that the impact would not have been so strong?

How

- How could you describe this experience to someone who found it hard to understand?
- How would it be for you if you were to know that she had not meant it in that way?
- How would you have liked it to have been different?

In what way

- In what way were your expectations met/not met?
- In what way might the thinking of both of you be blocking resolution?
- In what way has the other party managed this situation in a positive way?

What if...or If...?

- What if this had not happened, how would your relationship be now?

- What if he was to apologize to you, what might you offer in return?

- If you reached agreement at the end of the session, what would have been the contributory factor to this outcome?

BEWARE OF ASKING A WHY QUESTION

When a question beginning with Why is asked, the person being asked that question may feel that they should justify their opinions or actions. A Why question also invites defensiveness, justification and argument, and it may block cognitive thinking. Sometimes, there may seem to be only one answer to a Why question, and that is the answer in the mind of the questioner!

Figure: 7.3.
Put *Why* Behind Bars
CREDIT: O'SULLIVAN SOLUTIONS/
PAUL PIERSE

When a person is asked a question, particularly one that starts with Why, their amygdala searches their emotional memory store. If they perceive a threat, the person may turn to defense mechanisms for protection. In mediation, these defense mechanisms are most likely to manifest as denial, delusion, regression, withdrawal or aggression, with a party's position becoming more entrenched.

When a Why question is asked in a very gentle way with genuine curiosity, such as saying "I wonder why that happened?" then the response may not be one of justification or defense. However, the mediator's body language is crucial, and tone of voice needs to be gently curious and should focus on the issue and not the person.

Converting a Why Question into an Open Question

Why Question	Alternative Open Questions
Why did you come to that conclusion?	■ How did you come to that conclusion? ■ What influenced you to come to that conclusion?
Why did this go so badly wrong?	■ What is it that could have caused this outcome? ■ What are the things that did not help this situation?
Why did you do that?	■ What were the factors that brought you to the conclusion that this was the correct thing to do at that time? ■ When you did that, Tom, what were you hoping would happen?
Why don't you agree to what Karen is asking of you?	■ When Karen asks this of you, Tom, what are the concerns this may raise for you? ■ How might it be for you if you did agree to Karen's proposals, Tom? Or if you did not agree?

S3: The Seeking Information Dimension of Questions

S3: The Seeking Information Dimension of Questions

S3: The Seeking Information Dimension of Questions

Asking questions to seek information and clarification about S2:Subject Dimension of Questions:

People	Environment	Problem	PEP Interaction
	including the physical, social and psychological environment		How the People, the Environment and the Problem interact, influence and impact on each other

© www.osullivansolutions.ie

Figure: 8.1.

CREDIT: O'SULLIVAN SOLUTIONS

THE S3: SEEKING INFORMATION QUESTIONS strategically target the information that is required from the parties for the conversations needed for the mediation process. S3 questions directly seek information that may already be known or unknown by each of the parties. They also clarify existing information. S3 questions invite the party's perspective on the conflict. Creating a paradigm shift is not the intended goal when asking an S3 question, but it could be an unanticipated outcome.

When developing, and testing a hypothesis about what may be happening in a conflict between parties, an effective mediator needs to develop and ask questions that will also contradict their most likely hypothesis. If they only concentrate on looking for the information that confirms their hypothesis, then the amount of information gained will be limited.

The philosopher and statistician Nassim Nicholas Taleb, the Dean's Professor in the Sciences of Uncertainty at the University of Massachusetts at Amherst, explores this theory in *The Black Swan: The Impact of the Highly Improbable.* [35] This is how he describes a black swan:

> Firstly, it [a black swan] is an outlier, as it lies outside the realms of regular expectations, because nothing in the past can convincingly point to its possibility. Secondly, it carries an extreme impact. Thirdly, despite its outlier status, human nature makes us concoct explanations for its occurrence, after the fact, making it explainable and predictable.

To introduce as much information as possible, a mediator needs to be aware of this concept and the importance of looking for not only that which the parties don't know, but also that which the parties don't know they don't know. And the mediator needs to be actively open to asking searching questions to discredit their own hypothesis, in order to introduce as broad a range of information as possible into the mediation discussions.

S3: Seeking Information questions can be asked during all stages of the mediation process, but particularly at the start and during the storytelling stage, when the mediator is gathering information from the parties. The responses to these questions will form the pool of information about the conflict from which S4: Shift Thinking Dimension of questions can then be asked.

Examples of S3: Seeking Information Questions

S3: *Seeking Information Questions That* Clarify Existing Information

People

- You mention that you have not slept well since the start of the conflict, how did you sleep before this conflict? Specifically, what is it about the conflict that keeps you awake at night?
- You mentioned that Karen intrudes on your work; can you give me a specific example of what you mean?

Environment

- When you say that it all went wrong at that point, at what point specifically do you mean?
- Is it the context in which this happened that is concerning you the most, or is there a larger concern for you?
- What is it about that context that made it worse?

Problem

- Can you please define for me exactly what the problem is, so that I understand clearly?
- What is the cause of this problem?
- How does this problem compare to the problem that you described earlier in the session?

PEP Interaction

- When you say that the mood of those in the office changes when the manager is in the room, how does that dynamic change?
- What difference does this make for you?
- To what would you attribute this change?

The responses to these questions will form the pool of information about the conflict from which S4: Shift Thinking Dimension of Questions can be asked.

S3: Seeking Information Questions for Gathering New Information

Here are some examples of questions that will result in new information being heard by the parties.

People

- You say that this has been a tough time for you. Can you tell me a little bit more?
- How was your relationship at the time when you both started to work together?
- What contributed to your relationship breaking down? How did this impact on each of you?

Environment

- Can you give me an example of when/where/in what context this issue arises?
- What is it about this context that makes the conflict worse for you?
- What else contributes to it?
- What concerns you most about this?

Problem

- What is your understanding of the problem or issue?
- You say you had a good relationship with each other before this happened, what made this a problem for you?
- What makes the problem worse?

PEP Interaction

- How does the environment in which you are working contribute to the problem?
- How does this problem affect the organization and/or its productivity?
- What would others in the department say about your relationship and its impact on the organization?

Additional Techniques to Use with
S3: Seeking Information Questions

There are two additional techniques that can be coupled with S3: Seeking Information Questions:

1. Working with Metaphor

    Asking S3 Questions by incorporating any metaphors used by a party into the follow-up question

2. Clean Language

    Asking S3 Questions by using Clean Language

Both techniques facilitate a mediator to clarify existing information and uncover new information. These techniques are primarily designed to deliver clear and accurate information that connects specifically to the experiences of the parties. While the goal of these questions is to bring new information into the process, this in itself could create a paradigm shift.

1) S3 Questions Reflecting the Metaphors Used by a Party

Asking questions that include the metaphors used by the parties helps mediators to connect with a party's symbolic language so that the specifics of what a party is trying to voice can be clearly identified. The metaphors used by parties are their inner reality and can be the language of their unconscious minds. When metaphors are used by a party, they either communicate exactly that which was intended, or that which may have been intended, but is not yet conscious to the party. By repeating the metaphor used by a party, the mediator will help to maintain the party's link to their unconscious mind and potentially bring those thoughts to consciousness, if appropriate.

The purpose of working with metaphor in mediation is:

✓ To support parties to identify or voice the core of their experience.

✓ To facilitate a mediator and the other party to hear clearly what a party in mediation is trying to voice.

✓ To facilitate a party to make connections with other experiences when their feelings were similar (but only when appropriate to a mediation process), as this introduces context and perspective to their current issue.

✓ To support a party to move toward future agreement by using their metaphoric language in a way that connects specifically to their experiences, so that the solutions that are agreed are appropriate to those experiences.

Note:
Integrity and safety are key to working with metaphor, and the necessary precautions to take when asking this type of question are explained in this chapter. But prior to working with questions that incorporate a metaphor used by parties, it is important to know exactly what a metaphor is, and the potential challenges that can arise for mediators when working in this area. This section explains the meaning of the term metaphor, and how to work safely with metaphors during mediation process.

What Is a Metaphor?

In their book *Clean Language: Revealing Metaphors and Opening Minds*,[36] Wendy Sullivan and Judy Rees put forward some suggestions as to how to identify a metaphor:

1. If a sentence starts with words that describe the comparison of what a person is experiencing with something else, then it is a metaphor.

    Example:

    It's like…

    or

    It's as though…

    or

    It's as if…

2. If what is being described is referring to a different aspect of a person's life, it is probably a metaphor.

    Example:

    When a person is talking about their relationship with their boss and says:

    It's like when I used to have fights with my father...

    or

    It's like when I am traveling and someone pushes in front of me in the lineup...

3. If the words used refer to space or force, then it is probably a metaphor.

    Example:

    traveling along the bumpy road of life
    bringing it solidly back to ground...

4. If a person uses a sentence such as "We are standing at a crossroads," and if they are not standing at a crossroads, then this is a metaphor.

    Metaphors can be communicated in single words or through expressions or stories and can help a mediator understand a person's experience. Metaphors often reflect the interplay between our physical world and our thinking.

    Example of the use of a metaphor by a party in mediation:

    Negative metaphor: I feel a great weight on my back with this project.

    Positive metaphor: It is like the load has become lighter.

Precautionary Methods

The metaphors that are used for powerful, strong and deep negative emotions tend to be vivid and obvious and need to be managed very carefully by mediators, particularly those who are new to mediation practice or who are not sufficiently experienced in working with deep emotions.

USE SEPARATE PRIVATE MEETINGS TO IDENTIFY ANY VULNERABILITIES IN A PARTY

- A mediator needs to use the separate private meeting, before the joint meeting, to identify any deep negative emotions in a party so that these are not inadvertently exposed during the joint session.
- Do not work with or focus on metaphors that use *strong* negative emotions as this may evoke the deep emotional state of a party that is associated with those memories.

Examples of strong negative emotions that may signal deep distress or depression in a person are:

- I am in a *dark place* and I cannot get out of it. It is as if I have been *abused all over again* like when I was a child.

Should a mediator inadvertently delve into a party's powerful or deep negative emotions, then it is important to acknowledge what the party said, while using empathic body language and a slow, gentle and quiet tone of voice:

Mediator:

Karen, I hear you saying that you are in a *dark place* and that it is as if you have been *abused all over again* like when you were a child, and from what you are saying it looks like it has had a deep impact on you…
(Pause)
I am wondering what might need to happen to ensure that your expressed concerns about the future can be addressed appropriately so that you do not feel vulnerable at work?

However, there are many times when it can be useful and valuable to strategically deepen a strong emotion. For example, if a party says that they feel guilty or regretful about something they said or did during a conflict, then exploring these emotions at a deeper level will create understanding and acceptance between parties.

Using the metaphor that a party uses, and reflecting those exact words back to the them, indicates to a party that a mediator is deeply listening to, and hearing, what they are saying. The development of this rapport helps the mediator gain the trust of the party, which creates a climate where a party will feel encouraged to say openly and honestly what is affecting them in the conflict.

Examples of Questions for Using Metaphor with an S3 Question

Here is an example of a flow of questions that can be asked using a range of open questions from the S Questions Model.

SEEKING INFORMATION ABOUT WHAT THE PARTY IS EXPRESSING THROUGH METAPHOR

- Tom, you mentioned several times that you felt like tearing your hair out… May I ask you more about it, please? What do you mean specifically when you say that you felt you were tearing your hair out because of all this work?
- What is it like for you to feel that you are tearing your hair out with all this work?
- What do you feel is contributing to you feeling like tearing your hair out about this work?

MAKING CONNECTIONS WITH THE CONFLICT TRIGGER

- What exactly happened that led you to feel like you needed to tear your hair out?
- To what were you specifically reacting?
- What was happening for you before you felt like tearing your hair out?
- What were you thinking when you felt like tearing your hair out?
- What sort of things usually cause this reaction in you?

MAKING CONNECTIONS WITH OTHER CONTEXTS IN WHICH THE FEELING IS SIMILAR

- What were you worried or concerned about?
- With what is your feeling of tearing your hair out usually connected?
- Are there other situations when you feel like tearing your hair out?
- How is this experience similar or different?
- What were you thinking when you tore your hair out in other situations?
- What was distinctive about feeling like tearing your hair out this time?

SPECIFIC QUESTIONS TO ASK ABOUT THE OTHER PARTY

- At the time, what would have let the other person know that you felt like tearing your hair out?
- And what might the other person have been thinking, feeling, experiencing when you felt like tearing your hair out?
- When you reacted like you did, what do you think the other party thought that meant? How might their interpretation compare to what your intention had been?

2) S3 Questions Using Clean Language

This section will explore the use of the Clean Language question technique as a method for seeking information. This technique aims to ensure that a mediator's own perceptions, assumptions or bias do not taint the questions they pose.

Clean Language

Clean Language [37] questioning was created and developed by David Grove. What he aimed to do was quite specific: to introduce as few of his own assumptions and metaphors as possible, giving the client (or patient) maximum freedom for their own thinking. He didn't claim to be able to work *without influence or bias*, only that he aimed to minimize it. Clean Language questions facilitate parties to make connections with information related to their experience.

Wendy Sullivan and Judy Rees describe this further in their book *Clean Language*. The authors clearly and comprehensively illustrate the method for asking questions to ensure that the perceptions, assumptions or biases of the person asking the question do not influence the type of question they pose.

The Mediator's Assumptions

Despite our best intentions, mediators can sometimes include some of our own assumptions when we construct questions without using Clean Language. In the following example, the mediator's assumption was that the expectations of the party were the cause of the problem:

Party says:

I felt really *dragged down* after that.

Mediator:

How did your expectations contribute to you feeling *dragged down*?

On the other hand, using Clean Language ensures that any questions asked are justified by the logic of what a party has described. A Clean Language question is not tainted by a mediator's assumptions:

Party says:

I felt really *dragged down* after that.

Example of a mediator's Clean Language question that only uses the party's own words:

What kind of *dragged down* was that?

Was there anything else about that feeling of being *dragged down*?

Core or Basic Clean Language Questions

The core or basic Clean Language questions are divided into three categories; see the examples of each category in the table.

a) Developing questions

b) Sequence and source questions

c) Intention questions

Note:

In this sequence of questions, *X* means any specific words that the party uses in their conversation.

Core or Basic Clean Language Questions	The Purpose of Clean Language Questions
Developing Questions	
Developing questions facilitate a party to make connections with something else that they either know or have experienced previously.	
What kind of X (is that X)? Is there anything else about X? Where is X? and/or whereabouts is X? Is there a relationship between X and Y? When X… what happens to Y? That's X like what?	These questions draw out a descriptive narrative in a focused way by asking for a description of X. Regarding the question "Where is X?" the authors state that if there is something in someone's thoughts, then it is nearly certain to be located somewhere, but often we are not aware that our thoughts have locations in space.
Sequence and Source Questions	
These questions are asked about what happened before, during and after X happened. They allow parties to make connections with any missing information.	
Then what happens? What happens just before X? Where could X come from?	The purpose of "sequence and source" questions is to: a) Clarify the order and pattern in which things happen b) Clarify from where the symbol used (metaphor) comes c) Make connections with other information or experiences that may be relevant to the current experience of the party
Intention Questions	
These questions facilitate the party to think of what they would like for the future.	
What would X like to happen? What needs to happen for X? Can X (happen)?	These questions focus on solutions and the future.

Working with Metaphor Using Clean Language Questions

Developing Questions	
Mediator:	What is it about this issue that you would like to solve?
Party:	I would like to be able to push forward without the past problems I have had with Tom.
Mediator:	What kind of pushing forward?
Party:	Pushing forward without all the past tension between us. A healthy pushing forward.
Mediator:	Is there anything else about pushing forward?
Party:	Yes, I think it would bring us to a much better place, if we both decided to give it a try.
Mediator:	Whereabouts is that pushing forward?
Party:	It's right there in front of me. I can see it very clearly.
Mediator:	Is there a relationship between pushing forward and the concerns you raised earlier?
Party:	I think if we both push forward, Tom and I will create a much better working relationship. Then I think I will have the capacity to achieve a lot more in work as I won't be stressed all the time.
Mediator:	When you are pushing forward, what happens to Tom?
Party:	He is there pushing against me!
Mediator:	And that's like what?
Party:	Well, like we are fighting against each other all the time, instead of working in harmony.
Sequence and Source Questions	
Mediator:	Then what happens?
Party:	Well, the tension escalates, and we are both shouting at one another.
Mediator:	And then what happens?
Party:	I am afraid that the project will not get completed properly and I will be blamed.
Mediator:	Where could that come from?
Party:	When something like this happened before, I nearly lost my job and it was not my fault. It had a devastating impact on me.
Intention Questions	
Mediator:	And then what would you like to have happen with that pushing against you by Tom?
Party:	That Tom and I could push together in the same direction, and then we would both get our work done more effectively.
Mediator:	What needs to happen to achieve that?
Party:	We need to sit down and look at our job descriptions and work out where the overlap is. We need to do this with our supervisor. Then we need to look at some of the instances that have caused us to disagree with each other and see how they fit in with our updated job descriptions.
Mediator:	And then?
Party:	We need to talk about what we will do if we push against each other again. We need a backup plan.
Mediator:	And can that happen?
Party:	Yes, I need to talk with Tom about all this.

Section 4:

Practical Application of S4 Questions

Introduction: The Eight Types of S4: Shift Thinking Dimension of Questions

S4: The Shift Thinking Dimension of Questions

To uncover new information and insight, either by exploring and focusing thinking
or by connecting and expanding thinking, leading to a paradigm shift

Journey of Inference Questions
Interpretations, Assumptions, Conclusions, Beliefs, Actions

Purpose: To identify the link between interpretations and actions. To explore parties' current narratives and to shift perspectives toward a new narrative.

Neuro-linguistic Programming (NLP) Based Questions
Deletions, Distortions, Generalizations

Purpose: To bring clarity; explore subjective realities, explore bias and misinterpretations, and create congruency in communication.

Distinction and Difference Questions
People, Parts, Contexts, Opposites, Spatial, Comparisons, Time Span, Measurement or Ranking

Purpose: To bring clarity, relevance, measurement, boundary and a different perspective to the conflict.

Reflective Connecting Questions
Connecting with patterns and cycles of conflict, both intrapersonal and interpersonal, and in the broader context

Purpose: To raise awareness of negative patterns and cycles of conflict, to deconstruct past unhelpful patterns and to reconstruct new healthy patterns.

Cognitive Elements-based Questions
Knowledge; Opinion and Thinking; Beliefs, Values and Attitudes; Behaviour; Sense of Self/Identity; Environment

Purpose: To explore inner conflicts and inconsistencies between perception and reality, and between the six cognitive elements. To seek a paradigm shift that will restore cognitive consonance.

Other People Questions
Explore an imagined perspective of the other party, a third party, a cultural norm or hypothetical parties

Purpose: To open perspectives and create insight safely.

Underlying Interests Questions
Conflict Triggers, Impact, Beliefs, Values and Attitudes

Purpose: To move the conflict positions of the parties to the core of their conflict, and identify needs and underlying interests.

Future Focus Questions
Hypothetical, Conditional, Consequential, BATNA / MLATNA / WATNA

Purpose: To move parties off the conflict treadmill and facilitate cognitive thinking, leading to options and solutions.

Figure: 9.1.

CREDIT: O'SULLIVAN SOLUTIONS

The Overall Purpose of an
S4: Shift Thinking Dimension of Questions

An S4: SHIFT QUESTION helps introduce new information and insight to the parties and seeks to create a paradigm shift in their thinking and understanding. While an S3: Seeking Information question is a simple linear question that directly seeks information, an S4: Shift Question is a circular question and introduces deeper insight to the parties.

Summary S4 Questions

While S4 questions are presented in the S Questions Model in a certain order, this order is not rigid; each question can stand alone. But the general order of the questions moves from hearing what happened and how a party interpreted it and acted upon it, to distilling and exploring the information presented, to making connections with other experiences or events, to identifying any inner conflict or inconsistencies, to safely teasing out alternative perspectives, and finally to identifying the core of the problem and facilitating the creation of a future without the problems of the past. This is the journey through which parties may need to be facilitated. Each S4 category of question may be linked with each of the other seven categories of questions to achieve a specific outcome.

While the terms perspective, paradigm and paradigm shift have already been explained in Chapter 1, it is important to briefly review them again in the context of the introduction of S4: Shift Questions.

Paradigm and Perspective

A paradigm is how we see, interpret and understand our world and our role in it, and how we understand the roles of others. It is our view of the world and how it should be, and our model or template from which we make sense of our world. Our paradigm has been uniquely customized in line with our past experiences and the beliefs we have formed about ourselves, others and our world.

Our individual and unique paradigm is our reference point for interpreting information and giving meaning to what happens in it. It is a way of organizing, classifying and condensing sensory information to help us to understand our world.

Perspectives

Our paradigm influences our perspectives which, in turn, filter incoming information, so that we see and experience our world in the way we expect to see and experience it, according to our paradigm. Our filters are conditioned by our experiences as we learn about our surroundings throughout our lives. Paradigms often limit and color our perceptions and awareness, resulting in us finding it hard to see something that does not conform to our basic assumptions.

It is important to note that stored memories are memories of our perceptions or subjective realities, *not* memories of reality.

Paradigm Shift

When parties present at mediation their positions are often quite entrenched. This can be due to their conflicting perspectives. A paradigm shift occurs when parties hear each other and change their understanding, thinking and perspective about each other and about their conflict.

The questions asked during mediation aim to enable the parties to readjust their perspectives or subjective realities. The assumption here is that since subjective realities shape behaviors, then a readjustment of subjective realities might lead to a paradigm shift in thinking, and therefore, the readjustment of behaviors.

Creating a Paradigm Shift

As stated in Chapter 1, it is important to reiterate that our stored memories are memories of our perceptions or subjective realities, not memories of reality. When we react to a memory, we are reacting to the way we stored that memory. Supporting a party to think clearly and to make distinctions or connections in their thinking helps them to change the way they are storing that memory.

To create a paradigm shift in parties who are in conflict, mediators need to ask specific questions that explore and focus their thinking as well as connecting and expanding it.

Explore and Focus Thinking

These questions focus, narrow and explore the thinking of the parties so that they can distinguish differences, distil information, analyze their conflict clearly and identify their issues, needs and underlying interests.

Connect and Expand Thinking

These questions facilitate parties to generate connections in their brain with their existing experience and knowledge. They support a party to reflect on their conflict, as if from an external paradigm, and to generate connections with a possible future by expanding their thinking and teasing through future options.

Types of S4: Shift Thinking Dimension of Questions

The following chapters 10–17 will introduce the eight individual types of S4: Shift Thinking Dimension of questions. Each type of question has its own specific purpose but contributes to the overall purpose of these questions, which is to facilitate a party to gain new insight and to bring about a paradigm shift in their thinking and understanding.

The Eight Types of S4: Shift Thinking Questions

1. S4: Journey of Inference questions
2. S4: Neuro-linguistic Programming-based questions
3. S4: Cognitive Elements-based questions
4. S4: Distinction and Difference questions
5. S4: Reflective Connecting questions
6. S4: Other People questions
7. S4: Underlying Interests questions
8. S4: Future Focus questions

Each type of question is designed to focus attention on the subject under discussion and to ask questions that facilitate reflection, create insight and support action. While there are eight types of S4 questions and they are presented in the model in a certain order, each type is a stand-alone question with its own unique purpose. Each category may also be linked with any of the other seven categories of questions to achieve a specific outcome. It can also be interlinked with any of the other seven categories of questions to develop a combined S4 question, if required.

The rest of this section will introduce the eight types of S4: Shift Thinking questions, in eight consecutive chapters, under the following subheadings:

✓ What is this question?
✓ How do these questions work?
✓ When to ask these questions
✓ Methodology
✓ How do you build and ask this type of question? (with examples)

Hazard Warning

Template questions appropriate to specific situations are exampled for each of the question types. While these are presented as a flow of questions, this flow needs to be flexible to meet the needs of the parties and their discussions and should not be rigid.

10

**S4: The Shift Thinking Dimension of Questions —
Journey of Inference Questions**

S4: The Shift Thinking Dimension of Questions

To uncover new information and insight, either by exploring and focusing thinking or by connecting and expanding thinking, leading to a paradigm shift

Journey of Inference Questions
Interpretations, Assumptions, Conclusions, Beliefs, Actions

Purpose: To identify the link between interpretations and actions. To explore parties' current narratives and to shift perspectives toward a new narrative.

Neuro-linguistic Programming (NLP) Based Questions
Deletions, Distortions, Generalizations

Purpose: To bring clarity; explore subjective realities, explore bias and misinterpretations, and create congruency in communication.

Distinction and Difference Questions
People, Parts, Contexts, Opposites, Spatial, Comparisons, Time Span, Measurement or Ranking

Purpose: To bring clarity, relevance, measurement, boundary and a different perspective to the conflict.

Reflective Connecting Questions
Connecting with patterns and cycles of conflict, both intrapersonal and interpersonal, and in the broader context

Purpose: To raise awareness of negative patterns and cycles of conflict, to deconstruct past unhelpful patterns and to reconstruct new healthy patterns.

Cognitive Elements-based Questions
Knowledge; Opinion and Thinking; Beliefs, Values and Attitudes; Behaviour; Sense of Self/Identity; Environment

Purpose: To explore inner conflicts and inconsistencies between perception and reality, and between the six cognitive elements. To seek a paradigm shift that will restore cognitive consonance.

Other People Questions
Explore an imagined perspective of the other party, a third party, a cultural norm or hypothetical parties

Purpose: To open perspectives and create insight safely.

Underlying Interests Questions
Conflict Triggers, Impact, Beliefs, Values and Attitudes

Purpose: To move the conflict positions of the parties to the core of their conflict, and identify needs and underlying interests.

Future Focus Questions
Hypothetical, Conditional, Consequential, BATNA / MLATNA / WATNA

Purpose: To move parties off the conflict treadmill and facilitate cognitive thinking, leading to options and solutions.

Figure: 10.1.

CREDIT: O'SULLIVAN SOLUTIONS

S4: Journey of Inference Questions

JOURNEY OF INFERENCE QUESTIONS take a party through the information they selected during a precipitating event; the interpretations they made about that information; the assumptions they made; and the conclusions they then reached which, in turn, informed any decisions or actions they took. These questions also explore the beliefs of a party and how these beliefs may have influenced their Journey of Inference.

As described in Chapter 2, the decisions or actions of parties are governed by the amount and type of information their brains absorb and the emotions that surface for them while they are interpreting the limited amount of information they do process. Our brains tend to absorb information that affirms our own perspective and paradigm, and we seldom absorb information that challenges it.

The parties make their own unique Journeys of Inference based on their unique perspectives and beliefs. Journey of Inference questions are used to explore the thinking process that parties go through, usually unconsciously, to get from the experiencing of an event to their resulting judgments, decisions or actions.

Theoretical Background

Definitions of Interpretations, Assumptions, Conclusions and Beliefs

Interpretation	The action of explaining the meaning of something
Assumption	A thing that is accepted as true, or as certain to happen, without proof
Conclusion	A judgement or decision
Belief	A feeling that something is true, even though it may be unproven or irrational. Beliefs are built up over years, and they can influence assumptions. But assumptions cannot influence beliefs.

The Journey of Inference Takes Place in Our Mind

From the experience or event to the moment that a decision is made because of that experience, the journey of thinking takes place in the mind. Our understanding of the meaning of what happened, the assumptions we make, the conclusions we reach and the beliefs we form are all *thoughts* inside our mind.

The Journey of Inference

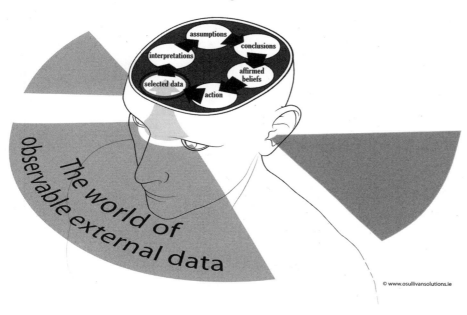

© www.osullivansolutions.ie

Figure: 10.2.
CREDIT: O'SULLIVAN SOLUTIONS

It is within this reality that we then live. In other words, we live inside the constraints of our own interpretation of the experience. If we do not possess finely tuned personal insight, and if we are not sufficiently emotionally intelligent, we may take this journey without any self-reflection, self-questioning or seeking any contradictory evidence.

> Most conflicts are triggered by external experiences, and information regarding them is conveyed to us by sensory inputs that have been gathered from our environment. Our conflicts therefore seem to us to take place externally, yet everything we understand about the meaning of what happened, and all our responses to the actions of others, are initiated and coordinated internally by the brains.
>
> — Kenneth Cloke [38]

Case study to illustrate a Journey of Inference

JOURNEY OF INFERENCE: STAFF IN A HOSPITAL LABORATORY

Ann and Mary have both worked in a hospital laboratory for five years. The laboratory had nine members of staff in total. The working relationship between Ann and Mary was good, and they even socialized together on occasions. Lately, however, Ann had noticed a slight difference in her relationship with Mary. There was nothing that she could specifically name — it was just a niggly feeling that Ann had had for a few weeks, with nothing to back it up.

Last week when Ann arrived at work, Mary was walking toward her in the hospital corridor. When Ann was about to say hello, she noticed that Mary kept her head down and did not say hello to her. Ann was taken aback by this and continued walking toward the laboratory. Ann's first thought was that this confirmed her previous suspicions: she interpreted the incident to mean that Mary wanted to avoid her, and she then assumed that Mary did not like her anymore and probably wished to end their friendship but had no idea why Mary would want to do this, especially without telling her why. As she continued to reflect, Ann became convinced that Mary had been talking about her behind her back to others in the laboratory. She concluded that all the people that Mary know won't want to have anything to do with her any more.

Ann then realized that this was just one more example of the way people behave: they never have the courage to say something to your face, but spend their time thinking negative thoughts about you, while continuing to smile and pretend that everything is OK with the friendship. Then they talk to others about you and try to turn them against you too. Ann immediately decided that she would stop talking to Mary and to all the other staff as well. Ann had experienced this situation many times before, and she believed that she knew exactly how to deal with it!

Over the next few days, both Mary and the other staff began to wonder what was wrong with Ann. But they did not approach her, because they noticed she was bubbling over with anger and they knew she could be aggressive at times. They did not want to create a scene, but they all engaged on their own individual Journeys of Inference and took actions in line with their personal past experiences and beliefs.

Over the following days, Ann noticed more and more things that confirmed her suspicion that no one wished to be her friend any more. She even started to proactively look for examples to prove that her beliefs were correct. The situation became steadily worse until one day Ann completely lost her temper with Mary in the hospital cafeteria while dozens of staff looked on. Mary went to the human resources department to make a complaint about Ann, and mediation was proposed.

The Journey of Inference

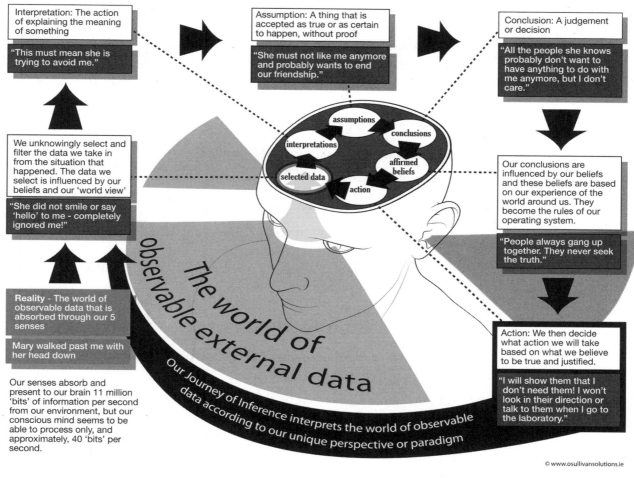

Figure: 10.3.

CREDIT: O'SULLIVAN SOLUTIONS

The Length of Time a Journey of Inference Takes

From the time that Mary walked past Ann in the corridor to the time Ann opened the door to enter the laboratory, less than a couple of seconds had passed. During that time, Ann interpreted the meaning of what had happened, made an assumption about that interpretation, reached a conclusion, checked how all this fitted in with her beliefs and decided what she was going to do about it. The more emotional a party becomes, the quicker they make their Journey of Inference and the more they believe that their inference is a true record of what happened.

Continuation and Escalation of the Conflict

Once the other party, such as Mary is this scenario, becomes aware of tension in the relationship, they start to make their own Journey of Inference. Each time one party acts, or omits to act, the other party to the conflict makes a further Journey of Inference. This in turn informs the actions that they take, and so the conflict becomes cyclical and escalates. As the conflict escalates, parties usually only observe the data that matches their previous beliefs and conclusions and bypass other observable data.

When parties in conflict act, they firmly believe that they are taking the correct action. Their positions then become more hardened and entrenched.

Background to the Development of the Journey of Inference

The concept of the "ladder of inference" was first developed by Chris Argyris and subsequently presented by Peter Senge in his book *The Fifth Discipline*.[39] In this book I am calling it the "Journey of Inference" because I consider it to be a continuous circular journey in the mind rather than a journey to the top of a ladder and back down again.

How Do Journey of Inference Questions Work?

Selecting data and making inferences is largely an unconscious process, but it can be made conscious through mediation questions. Supporting parties to be aware of the limited information from which they made their inferences and assumptions, and then reached their conclusions, is vital to the creation of mutual understanding. Journey of Inference questions facilitate the identification of what triggered a party's reaction as well as their subsequent interpretations and the adoption of their positions.

When links are made between a party's interpretations and their resultant actions, that can help to explain the rationale behind their behavior. Asking a party about how they perceived and interpreted an action by the other, and then comparing this with the actual intention of that party who took the action, also serves to bring new information and insight to a mediation process.

Journey of Inference questions support parties to look for new and clarifying information that may even prove their interpretations and assumptions to have been incorrect. The resulting reinterpretations they make may then be more accurate and balanced.

Note:
Eric E. Vogt, in *The Art and Architecture of Powerful Questions,* [40] asks what happens to assumptions through the incisive articulation of powerful questions. Vogt concludes that questions may have one of the following four impacts upon assumptions:

- They may reinforce existing assumptions.
- They may create new assumptions.
- They may alter previously held assumptions.
- They may destroy existing assumptions.

Vogt states that it is much easier to reinforce someone's prevailing assumption than to alter it — this is the challenge for mediators when taking a party through Journey of Inference questions.

When to Ask Journey of Inference Questions

These questions are used:

✓ When there is a need to identify and explore the point in time when a party adopted their position about their conflict (conflict trigger), or when the conflict escalated

✓ When exploration of a party's thought process would lead to greater understanding between parties

✓ When parties do not understand the behavior of the other party

✓ When parties are intransigent about their positions

✓ When a party states that they know exactly what the intentions of the other party were, and when you, as the mediator, have heard differently

> Parties demonstrate this with statements such as:

> > I know exactly what she was trying to do …

> > Obviously, she did it because …

> > Well it is very clear to me that …

✓ When parties do not differentiate between their opinions and facts and put forward an opinion as being a fact

✓ When conflict has escalated and each party's actions are influenced by what the other party said or did, leading to a circular conflict dynamic

✓ When facilitating a party's expression of regret by asking questions about what they would have done differently if they had had the information and insight learned during the mediation discussion

Methodology

While Chapter 4 contains generic guidelines for asking questions, additional specific guidelines for asking Journey of Inference questions are set out here.

Guidelines for Asking Journey of Inference Questions

✓ Journey of Inference questions should be asked only after the parties have told their story. To ask them before or during this initial storytelling may appear analytical and judgmental.

✓ Each party may be asked about his or her Journey of Inference from beginning to end:

or

✓ The parties may be asked in turn about their interpretations, then about their assumptions, and so on. But this latter method requires very tight facilitation.

✓ After a party's response, and prior to asking the next question, a mediator sometimes needs to reflect back what they have heard so that the party does not feel like they are being interrogated.

✓ Parties may find it challenging to differentiate between interpretations and assumptions. One way to counteract this is to first ask, "What did you think that X meant?" when asking about interpretations, and then, "And what did you then think that would mean?" for assumptions.

✓ A party can be asked about his or her own Journey of Inference and then be asked to hypothesize about the other party's Journey of Inference. This can be helpful in a joint meeting if one party claims that the other party does not understand them, but when you as the mediator know differently.

✓ The Journey of Inference questioning process can stop at any time, if necessary, for example:

- If understanding is reached early in the questioning process — for instance, at interpretations stage.
- If one party is finding the process too intense and difficult.

The Steps Involved in Asking Journey of Inference Questions

There are three steps involved in developing a series of Journey of Inference questions:

> Step 1: Hearing the narrative of a party
> Step 2: Challenging the narrative
> Step 3: Building a possible new narrative

Questioning Tasks	Stages of a Journey of Inference
Step 1 Hearing the narrative of a party Exploring and focusing thinking for each of the stages of the Journey of Inference And **Step 2** Challenging the narrative Connecting and expanding the thinking of a party about each stage of the Journey of Inference	**Stage 1:** The consciously or unconsciously selected data **Stage 2:** The interpretations made from the data selected **Stage 3:** The assumptions formed because of the interpretations made **Stage 4:** The conclusions or judgments reached **Stage 5:** How the judgments and conclusions were informed by the beliefs of the party **Stage 6:** The decisions or actions taken because of the beliefs of the party about the situation
Step 3 Building a possible new narrative Connecting and expanding thinking	When the past has been deconstructed, and it appears, or is stated, that new learning and insight have been gained, it is time to start creating a new narrative with possibilities for agreement. A review of the process may be done intermittently, both during the Journey of Inference question flow and at the end of the process.

Note:

If a paradigm shift has occurred after any stage of the Journey of Inference, then there may not be a need to continue with questions, unless further understanding is needed by the parties.

Step 1: Hearing the Narrative

S3: Seeking Information questions need to be asked about the Journey of Inference made by a party: what did they see, how did they interpret what they saw, what assumptions did they make, what conclusions did they reach, on what beliefs were their conclusions based, and what decisions or actions did they take? The goal during Step 1 is to uncover new information but not necessarily to create a paradigm shift, although one may result.

EXPLORING AND FOCUSING THINKING ON THE JOURNEY OF INFERENCE
MADE — HEARING THE NARRATIVE

The case study of Ann and Mary is used for the flow of questions here. This example focuses only on Ann's Journey of Inference, but in real practice Mary would be asked similar questions.

The Event
- Ann, would you like to tell me what happened, please, when you and Mary passed each other in the corridor? Then what happened?

Selected Data
- What did you observe, Ann? What information or facts did you take from this event?

Interpretations
- When that happened [Mary walking past you with her head down], what did you think it meant? What brought you to this interpretation?

Assumptions
- And what did you think that meant, and what assumptions did you make about what might happen? What brought you to that assumption?

Conclusions and Judgments
- After you made that assumption, what conclusions or judgments did you come to? What brought you to this judgment or conclusion?

Beliefs
- What are your beliefs about the world and how people usually behave in a situation like this?

Actions
- How did these beliefs influence the decisions you made or the actions you took afterwards? What did you decide to do?
- And then what happened? What else happened?

Note:
After going through Step 1, mediators need to summarize, identify and name to parties the link between the initial interpretations made by a party and the resulting decisions or actions they took.

Step 2: Challenging the Narrative

CHALLENGING THE NARRATIVE BY CONNECTING AND EXPANDING THINKING ABOUT
THE JOURNEY OF INFERENCE

Selected Data

- What had you been thinking/feeling about Mary before/when this happened?
- On what did you base that thinking? What was the tangible evidence for this?
- What had been your expectations of Mary? What influenced those expectations?
- If you had not been concentrating on what you were expecting, what else might you have seen?
- What would others have observed if they had been there when Mary walked past you with her head down?
- When this happened, what did this trigger in you? What was going on for you inside?
- And how could your sense of insecurity about the friendship have influenced what you saw/did not see?
- What are the things you may have missed?
- On a scale of 0 to 10, with 10 indicating complete certainty, how certain can you be about...?
- What is this uncertainty about? (If the response is less than 10)

Interpretations

- Ann, what did you think might have been Mary's intention?
- What influenced or contributed to you interpreting what you observed in this way?
- How might your stated niggly feeling about your friendship with Mary have influenced what you actually saw and your interpretations? If your friendship had still been good when Mary passed you in the corridor with her head down, what might your interpretations have been?
- What are all the questions you have been asking yourself since this happened?
- Hypothetically, if you had made an interpretation opposite to the one you made, what may have been the result?

- If you were to look at yourself and this incident from a balcony, what might you have seen and what interpretations might you have made?
- If I was to ask you to prove yourself wrong, what evidence would there be to support this?
- At this stage, on a scale of 0 to 10, with 10 indicating complete certainty, how certain are you of your initial interpretation?
- Tell me about the bit of uncertainty that you mentioned. What is this uncertainty about?
- Is there a time or a circumstance that might result in you interpreting this differently?

Questions can also be asked about the perspective of the other party:

- If asked, what might Mary say about the time you saw her passing you in the hospital corridor?
- What do you think would surprise Mary the most about what you interpreted from this situation, and about what you mentioned about her intent?
- What interpretation might Mary have liked you to make?

If a mediator knows that Ann's inferences about Mary were not in line with the stated intentions of Mary, then ask:

- Ann, if you were to hear that Mary had not actually meant that in the way that you interpreted it, and if she were to say that she regretted what happened afterwards because she valued your friendship, how would that affect the way you interpret it?

At this stage there may be sufficient insight created with Ann and no need to continue, but if this is not the case, then continue asking questions about the rest of the stages of a Journey of Inference:

Assumptions

- What assumptions did you make after you initially interpreted Mary's actions in that way?
- What did you think was going to happen?
- What influenced you to make this specific assumption?
- What other assumptions could you have made?
- If you had made a different assumption, what might have been the outcome?

The mediator may continue with more questions about the assumptions made, based on Ann's responses if relevant.

Conclusions

- After you made that initial assumption, what judgment or conclusion did you come to, Ann?
- What brought you to make this judgment or conclusion? What did this decision mean for you?
- What other conclusions could you have come to?
- If you were to try to persuade yourself that this conclusion was incorrect, how would you do this, and what evidence might there be to support this hypothetical conclusion?
- What might have happened if you had come to different conclusions?

The mediator may continue with more questions about the conclusions made, and ask the party to rank their alternative conclusions, if relevant.

Beliefs

- What is it you think or believe about life or people that brought you to that conclusion? How has this belief served you in the past? Are there situations where these beliefs may be valid or invalid? What are the distinctions you make between these situations?
- What other beliefs do you have that could have resulted in your reaching a different conclusion?
- Reflecting on the thoughts you have just expressed, if you had interpreted what you saw differently, and if you had reached a different conclusion, how would that have fitted in with your beliefs about the world and about how people usually behave in a situation like this?
- What thoughts or reflections is this raising for you?

Actions

- You mentioned earlier that after this event you made decisions about how you were going to respond to it and that the conflict escalated and you felt more entrenched. Having reflected on this now, what other decisions or actions could you have taken?
- How might this have impacted on the conflict situation and its progression?
- What might have been the outcomes?

Note:

To broaden the perspective and expand the thinking of a party, asking S4: Journey of Inference questions from a third-party perspective is valuable. These are called S4: Other People questions and are described in Chapter 15. These questions can be asked at any stage of a Journey of Inference and will prompt the party to question whether their interpretation may have been linked to their perceptions and expectations rather than to reality.

Examples:

- If others had been present, what might they have observed?
- How might someone else have interpreted this?
- What might Mary have observed about herself that day?
- What might Mary say about not lifting her head up and saying hello?
- What might Mary have observed about you?

At times, only one party needs to be asked Journey of Inference questions. But in this case, Mary had also made a Journey of Inference, so similar questions needed to be asked of her.

During this flow of questions, Mary said she had not even noticed Ann in the corridor that morning, but she had certainly noticed the mood that Ann was in when she entered the lab because other staff had noted it too (data selected).

Mary said she remembered this morning clearly as she and her husband had just had another huge row before she came to work that morning. Mary went on to say that things had not been good between herself and her husband recently, and she had slowly been coming to the realization over the last few months that her marriage was ending, but after that morning's row, she said she became convinced that separation was the only answer.

Mary said she was upset by this bad humor of Ann's even though she knew she had been engrossed in her own problems and had not been chatting to Ann as much as usual. But Mary said she did not think that Ann's bad mood that morning had anything to do with her, as Ann displayed the same negative behavior toward all the other staff (interpretation). Because of this, Mary thought the problem would get sorted out by someone else in the end (assumption).

Mary said she remembered reflecting that this problem with Ann was coming on top of her marriage problems, and she did not have the energy to do anything but concentrate on her own marital problems (conclusion). Mary said that if she had not been so troubled already, she would have chatted with Ann to see what was wrong with her that morning, as she really felt it was important to be honest and talk about things face to face (belief). But she said she was too engrossed in her own marital worries at the time.

But Mary said that as time went on, she slowly started to surmise that maybe Ann did have a specific problem with her, and when Ann lost her temper with her in the hospital cafeteria this was confirmed — with a bang! Mary said that after that happened she went to the HR department to make a complaint against Ann, as she felt completely humiliated by Ann's public display of temper toward her (action).

Step 3: Building a Possible New Narrative

CONNECTING AND EXPANDING THINKING

When the past has been deconstructed and it appears, or is stated, that new learning and insight have been gained by both parties, then it is time to start reflecting on any further misinterpretations that parties may have made.

- Mary and Ann, as the conflict progressed, what do you think each of you may have intended that may have been misinterpreted by the other?

- What do each of you think your misinterpretation may have meant for the other party?

- In what way might this interpretation have led to either of you employing a particular behavior as a response?

Creating understanding between the parties is further helped by facilitating them to talk about the impact that the conflict is having on them. This may only be done if a mediator knows that each party will listen to the other respectfully.

- How has this conflict impacted on both of you?
- What has been the worst thing for each of you in all this?
- How did the impact of all this influence the thinking of both of you and the actions you took?
- With what kinds of things do you think the other party struggled?
- What do each of you need the other person to know or understand now?
- What might each of you have needed for this to happen differently?
- What could each of you now offer the other?

FACILITATING REGRET AND USING THE PAST TO INFORM THE FUTURE

If there has been a paradigm shift in one or both parties, then the following questions may allow for some regret to be shown and may open possibilities for solutions.

- If you were to go back in time with the information that you have now, what might each of you have said/done differently?

STATEMENT OF THE NEW NARRATIVE

- If you were to tell this story now to another person, based on the understanding you have both gained, how would you describe this story to them?

Note:

Further issues may arise here and may need to be managed.

Note:

This embeds the initiation of the new narrative.

AGREEMENTS REGARDING THE FUTURE

- If something like this were to happen again, how would you manage it? What would each of you need from the other? What could each of you offer the other?

- What can be taken from your learning to inform agreements between you for the future?

Reviewing Progress Through Journey of Inference Stages

REVIEWING PROGRESS DURING THE PROCESS OF ASKING JOURNEY OF INFERENCE QUESTIONS:

At any stage of the Journey of Inference questioning process, parties can be asked about:

- The process that is being used

- Whether they have gained any new information or insight

- The impact of this new information or insight on their thinking or approach

- Whether, in retrospect, they would have done anything differently. This could facilitate some regret and help the parties to bring this learning into a future agreement.

REVIEWING PROGRESS AT THE CONCLUSION OF THE PROCESS OF ASKING JOURNEY OF INFERENCE QUESTIONS:

Examples of questions:

- What was it like for you to go through that thinking process?

- Is there anything else that you may not have said that the other person does not know?

- What have you not discussed that you might still need to talk about with each other?

- What has changed for you because of this process?

- What may have influenced or contributed to your change in thinking?

- What might you now need from each other to continue this process?

- What would you like to offer each other?

Key Learning

JOURNEY OF INFERENCE QUESTIONS

Journey of Inference questions take a party through the information they selected during an event; the interpretations they made about that information; the assumptions they made; and the conclusions they then reached, which, in turn, informed any decisions or actions they took. These questions also explore the beliefs of a party and how these beliefs may have influenced that party's Journey of Inference.

STEP 1

Hear the narrative of the parties

Ask S3: Seeking Information questions about the Journey of Inference made by a party: what did they see, how did they interpret what they saw, what assumptions did they make, what conclusions did they reach, on what beliefs were their conclusions based, and what decisions or actions did they take? The goal during Step 1 is to get new information but not necessarily to create a paradigm shift, although one may result.

STEP 2

Challenge the narrative

Ask questions that will support parties to make connections and expand their thinking about each stage of the Journey of Inference.

STEP 3

Build a possible new narrative

Connect and expand thinking and construct a possible new narrative — when the past has been deconstructed and it appears, or is stated, that new learning and insight have been gained, then it is time to start reconstructing a future with a new narrative and possibilities for agreement.

REVIEW PROGRESS

As needed, review progress and check in with the parties about the process used, during the process and/or at its completion.

Hazard Warning

Do not pressure a party to answer a question — proceed carefully and gently, at their pace, and with their permission.

**S4: The Shift Thinking Dimension of Questions —
Neuro-linguistic Programming Questions**

S4: The Shift Thinking Dimension of Questions

To uncover new information and insight, either by exploring and focusing thinking
or by connecting and expanding thinking, leading to a paradigm shift

Journey of Inference Questions
Interpretations, Assumptions, Conclusions, Beliefs, Actions

*Purpose: To identify the link between interpretations and actions.
To explore parties' current narratives and to shift perspectives
toward a new narrative.*

Neuro-linguistic Programming (NLP) Based Questions
Deletions, Distortions, Generalizations

*Purpose: To bring clarity; explore subjective realities,
explore bias and misinterpretations, and create congruency
in communication.*

Distinction and Difference Questions
People, Parts, Contexts, Opposites, Spatial, Comparisons,
Time Span, Measurement or Ranking

*Purpose: To bring clarity, relevance, measurement, boundary
and a different perspective to the conflict.*

Reflective Connecting Questions
Connecting with patterns and cycles of conflict, both
intrapersonal and interpersonal, and in the broader context

*Purpose: To raise awareness of negative patterns and
cycles of conflict, to deconstruct past unhelpful patterns
and to reconstruct new healthy patterns.*

Cognitive Elements-based Questions
Knowledge; Opinion and Thinking; Beliefs, Values and Attitudes;
Behaviour; Sense of Self/Identity; Environment

*Purpose: To explore inner conflicts and inconsistencies between
perception and reality, and between the six cognitive elements.
To seek a paradigm shift that will restore cognitive consonance.*

Other People Questions
Explore an imagined perspective of the other party, a third party,
a cultural norm or hypothetical parties

Purpose: To open perspectives and create insight safely.

Underlying Interests Questions
Conflict Triggers, Impact, Beliefs, Values and Attitudes

*Purpose: To move the conflict positions of the parties to the core
of their conflict, and identify needs and underlying interests.*

Future Focus Questions
Hypothetical, Conditional, Consequential,
BATNA / MLATNA / WATNA

*Purpose: To move parties off the conflict treadmill and facilitate
cognitive thinking, leading to options and solutions.*

Figure: 11.1.
CREDIT: O'SULLIVAN SOLUTIONS

S4: Neuro-linguistic Programming-based Questions

(Refer to Chapter 2 for further background theory on Neuro-Linguistic Programming)

NEURO-LINGUISTIC PROGRAMMING ENCOMPASSES the three most influential components involved in producing human experience: neurology, language and programming. The NLP model of communication is a tool for understanding how people process incoming information through their uniquely created filters, and then communicate that information to others. NLP-based questions distill and diagnose issues, explore and challenge subjective realities, explore bias and misinterpretations and create congruency between the statements of a party and what the party really means.

Theoretical Background

NLP theory states that we consciously or unconsciously delete, distort and generalize our experiences in line with our paradigm or view of the world. And the process by which we limit and distort our representation of our world to ourselves is the same process by which we limit and distort our expression of our world to others.

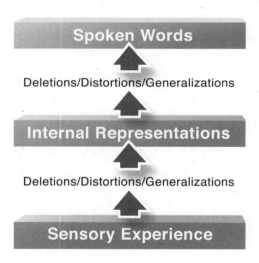

Figure: 11.2.

According to Robert Dilts,[41] NLP is founded on two fundamental suppositions:

1. The Map Is Not the Territory

   As human beings, we can never know reality. We can only know our perceptions of reality. We experience and respond to the world around us primarily through our sensory representational systems. It is our "neuro-linguistic" maps of reality that determine how we behave and that give those behaviors meaning, not reality itself. It is generally not reality that limits us or empowers us, but rather our map of reality.

2. Life and "Mind" Are Systemic Processes

   The processes that take place within a human being, and between human beings and their environment, are systemic. Our bodies, our societies and our universe form an ecology of complex systems and subsystems, all of which interact with and mutually influence each other. It is not possible to completely isolate any part of the system from the rest of the system. Such systems are based on certain "self-organizing" principles and naturally seek optimal states of balance or homeostasis.

   This need to seek balance or homeostasis is also covered in the theory of cognitive dissonance in Chapter 14: Cognitive Elements Questions.

How Do Neuro-linguistic Programming Questions Work?

NLP-based questions challenge a party's subjective view of the world and distil and diagnose their issues. By asking NLP Meta Model-based questions, a mediator reconnects the deletions, distortions and generalizations voiced by the parties with the experience that created them. This facilitates them to move toward being congruent between what they think and what they say to the other party. The more aligned parties are with what they say and what they truly mean, the more coherent will be their message. The less coherent they are, the less their communication will be understood by the other party.

The focus of these questions opens subtle differences in the thinking of a party and invites a diagnosis of a party's statement, with a resulting shift in their perspective. Working on the assumption that subjective realities shape behaviors, a readjustment of subjective realities could lead to a paradigm shift in the thinking of the parties, resulting in a readjustment of their behaviors.

When to Ask Neuro-linguistic Programming-based Questions?

These questions are used:

✓ To identify and explore any subjective interpretations or subjective assumptions

✓ When the subjective realities of the parties are a block to creating understanding or progress

✓ When there is a need to differentiate between opinions and facts as stated by parties

✓ When it seems that information has been either consciously or unconsciously omitted by the parties

✓ When distorted or generalized information needs to be clarified or distilled

✓ To facilitate parties to be congruent in their thinking and their statements

✓ To create opportunities to minimize blame on both sides

✓ When uncovering the positive intent of a party will lead to understanding by the other party

✓ To recognize and remove blocks to progress and agreement

Methodology

In her book *NLP at Work: The Difference that Makes the Difference in Business*, Sue Knight breaks the types of deletions, distortions and generalizations people make into sub-elements, which provide the base for focused mediation questions. These questions need to be diagnostic in their approach and focus specifically on what a party has said.

NLP Meta Model Types That Form the Base for Building an NLP Question

NLP Meta Model *Elements of NLP Deletions, Distortions and Generalizations*		
1. Deletions	**2. Distortions**	**3. Generalizations**
Deletions: sub-elements a) Comparisons b) Vague subjects, actions and references c) Abstractions or nominalizations	Distortions: sub-elements a) Blamers or cause and effect b) Mind reading c) Interpretation or complex equivalent d) Presupposition e) Opinion as facts or "absolutist" pronouncements	Generalizations: sub-elements a) Universal statements b) Stoppers and limiters c) Drivers

Deletions, Distortions and Generalizations

This section will illustrate a menu of questions that can be asked about the NLP Meta Model categories of deletion, distortion and generalizations.

The questions need to be posed in a very gentle, unobtrusive and non-judgmental manner.

1. Deletions

Deletion occurs when we omit, or pay attention only to, certain aspects of the information represented to our brain through our senses. We absorb that which affirms our unique perception or paradigm and filter out the remaining information, as we either do not think it relevant or important or did not see it in the first place. Deletion is essential if we are not to become overwhelmed by the amount of information constantly available to us. The deletion process is often unconscious and can result in the omission of important information from a mediation process.

Note:
Many of the questions needed for checking a party's Journey of Inference can be NLP-based, particularly those that work with any interpretations made by a party.

Element of Deletions: Comparisons

An experience cannot be interpreted from a vacuum. It needs to be referenced to something else so that there is a benchmark from which to describe it. Mediators need to find out what that benchmark may be so that the comment can be reframed more specifically and appropriately.

Statement

She is a terrible manager!

Meta Model Questions

When you say *terrible*, what exactly do you mean? Terrible in relation to? Is she this way on some occasions or on all occasions? What has been your experience of managers? How does this manager compare to other managers you have worked with? What specifically is different? What is similar?

Element of Deletions: Vague Subjects, Actions and References

Deletions can occur when the identity of a person or the meaning of what they said is not conveyed clearly.

Statement

It is impossible to deal with them! They just do not care!

Meta Model Questions

What is impossible to deal with? With whom is it impossible to deal? When you say "impossible," what do you mean? Is it all of it or parts of it that are impossible? What do you mean when you use the word "deal"? How do people usually deal with this? What is it that you mean when you say "they do not care"? What is it that they do not care about? How do they show that they do not care?

Element of Deletions: Abstractions or Nominalizations

When a verb is removed from a sentence and replaced with a noun — a process called nominalization — this can make a problem seem intractable. The mediator needs to respond with a question that turns the noun back into a verb so that specific information can be gained. Then the complaint will become more specific and seem easier to address rather than seeming like an all-encompassing and dramatic "no hope at all" statement.

Statement

Our communication is terrible!

Meta Model Questions

What is not working about the way you communicate with each other? What way would you like to communicate instead?

2. Distortions

We change our experience of something by distorting the way in which we absorb information, or relay that information to others. We may blow something out of proportion or diminish it; we may alter a sequence of events; or make interpretations or assumptions, or jump to conclusions about something, without evidence. When we distort the information we process at a conscious level, then our experience of a situation will be a distorted experience.

Element of Distortions: Blamers or Cause and Effect

Blamers, or cause and effect language, can be used by a party who does not take responsibility for their own responses and reactions to what another person says or does. Instead of focusing on the person about whom the complaint is being made, focus on the resulting emotion.

Statement

She made me so angry!

Meta Model Questions

To what were you responding with anger?
What specifically triggered this anger in you?
What was it exactly that you were angry about?

Element of Distortions: Mind Reading

A party may make statements in which they assume to know what the other party is thinking or feeling.

Statement

She knows that this is important to me!

Meta Model Questions

What exactly makes you say that she knows this is important to you?
How have you impressed on her the importance of this to you?

This type of question can also be used when posing S4: Journey of Inference questions.

Note:

Questions for exploring distortions can also be used when posing S4: Journey of Inference questions.

Example:
We apply interpretation to what we hear, without first checking it out —

Statement
She does this all the time, so she does not care about anyone.

Meta Model Questions
What is it about the way she behaves that makes you think she does not care about anyone?

Element of Distortions: Interpretation or Complex Equivalent A = B

This is when a party attributes meaning to what another says or does.

> Statement
>> She spoke to me in a sharp way, so that must mean she is angry with me.

> Meta Model Questions
>> What is it that brings you to link the way she spoke to you with the fact that she is angry with you?
>> What was it about the way she spoke to you that results in you saying that?

Element of Distortions: Presupposition

When a limiting assumption is implied but is not said directly. For example, during a mediation with his supervisor, Karen, Tom asks her why he has not been given the responsibilities that are in his job description.

> Statement from supervisor, Karen
>> I asked another staff member to take on that responsibility as I thought Tom was too busy.

> Meta Model Questions
>> Karen, what made you think that Tom was too busy?
>> What did you hear that brought you to the conclusions that Tom was too busy?

Element of Distortions: Opinion as Facts or Absolutist Pronouncements

This occurs when an individual interprets their perception of the world as being reality or the only truth. They give an opinion as an absolute fact rather than an opinion and assume that their perspective is the truth. The person is unaware that each of us has different experiences and therefore different perspectives, and that our memories are of our perceptions rather than facts.

> Statement
>> He is rewriting history; that is not the way it happened! I know the truth!

> Meta Model Questions
>> What exactly is it that you know?
>> What is the truth from your perspective?
>> What might be the truth from the other party's perspective?

This type of question can also be incorporated into S4: Journey of Inference questions.

3. Generalizations

Generalizations are when we take a specific experience, draw universal assumptions about it and then apply them as true to everything outside the context of that specific experience. We can have an opinion of one person and then apply it to a whole category or race of people. Our beliefs then become generalizations and give us ways of predicting the world based on what we have experienced previously. We expect that our future will fit into this pattern and we only look for the information that will confirm our beliefs. We can even generalize a specific problem to our entire life and so detach ourselves from the real experience and the possibility of a different experience.

Element of Generalizations: Universal Statements

When a person takes an example of behavior and then draws conclusions that apply to everyone in that community, or that apply to all that person's actions, this is a generalization. When a person is generalizing, they use absolutist language and often include words such as *always, never, they all* or *no one* in their sentences.

> Statement
>> All immigrants are like that....

> Meta Model Questions
>> What makes you say that *all* immigrants are like that?
>> What experience have you had that leads you to say that?
>> Could there be some immigrants who are not like that?

> Statement
>> He is always like that...

> Meta Model Questions
>> Is there ever a time when he is not like that?

Element of Generalizations: Stoppers and Limiters

These statements stop and limit opportunities and possibilities. Phrases such as *I can't, I am not able to* and *That could never work!* are used. These statements need to be translated into a positive possibility.

> Statement
>> That could never happen....

> Meta Model Questions
>> What could help to make it happen?

Element of Generalizations: Drivers

These are the pressures we internalize that drive our thoughts and actions. These statements include words such as *should, must* or *have to* in their composition.

Statement

They must do this the way I say it should be done.

Meta Model Questions

What causes you to say that?

What might that deliver for you?

What might it be like if they do it in a way that is different?

Key Learning

NEURO-LINGUISTIC PROGRAMMING-BASED QUESTIONS

NLP-based questions distill and diagnose issues; explore and challenge subjective realities, biases and misinterpretations and create congruency between the statements of a party and what they really mean. To support someone in adjusting their subjective realities means asking questions that will first help them to distil and focus their existing information.

Asking questions pertaining to what the parties may have deleted, distorted or generalized in their interpretation of events, and in their communication of it to others, opens subtle differences in their thinking, expands their subjective view of the world, uncovers new information and creates new insight.

In her book *NLP at Work*, Sue Knight breaks the types of deletions, distortions and generalizations that people make into sub-elements that provide the base for asking focused mediation questions. These questions need to be diagnostic in their approach and focus specifically on what a party has said, so that they can be congruent in their message to the other party.

NLP Meta Model Types That Form the Base for Building an NLP Question

NLP Meta Model Elements of NLP Deletions, Distortions and Generalizations		
1. Deletions	**2. Distortions**	**3. Generalizations**
Deletions: sub-elements a) Comparisons b) Vague subjects, actions and references c) Abstractions or nominalizations	Distortions: sub-elements a) Blamers or cause and effect b) Mind reading c) Interpretation or complex equivalent d) Presupposition e) Opinion as facts or "absolutist" pronouncements	Generalizations: sub-elements a) Universal statements b) Stoppers and limiters c) Drivers

Hazard Warning

It is important to reiterate here that, if necessary for the safety of a party, these questions may need to be tested during the initial separate private meeting or in a private meeting during a joint session.

Hazard Warning

Do not pressure a party to answer a question — proceed carefully and gently, at their pace, and with their permission. NLP-based questions can be quite interrogative unless asked gently.

S4: Distinction and Difference Questions

**S4: The Shift Thinking Dimension of Questions —
Distinction and Difference Questions**

S4: The Shift Thinking Dimension of Questions

**To uncover new information and insight, either by exploring and focusing thinking
or by connecting and expanding thinking, leading to a paradigm shift**

Journey of Inference Questions
Interpretations, Assumptions, Conclusions, Beliefs, Actions

*Purpose: To identify the link between interpretations and actions.
To explore parties' current narratives and to shift perspectives
toward a new narrative.*

Neuro-linguistic Programming (NLP) Based Questions
Deletions, Distortions, Generalizations

*Purpose: To bring clarity; explore subjective realities,
explore bias and misinterpretations, and create congruency
in communication.*

Distinction and Difference Questions
People, Parts, Contexts, Opposites, Spatial, Comparisons,
Time Span, Measurement or Ranking

*Purpose: To bring clarity, relevance, measurement, boundary
and a different perspective to the conflict.*

Reflective Connecting Questions
Connecting with patterns and cycles of conflict, both
intrapersonal and interpersonal, and in the broader context

*Purpose: To raise awareness of negative patterns and
cycles of conflict, to deconstruct past unhelpful patterns
and to reconstruct new healthy patterns.*

Cognitive Elements-based Questions
Knowledge; Opinion and Thinking; Beliefs, Values and Attitudes;
Behaviour; Sense of Self/Identity; Environment

*Purpose: To explore inner conflicts and inconsistencies between
perception and reality, and between the six cognitive elements.
To seek a paradigm shift that will restore cognitive consonance.*

Other People Questions
Explore an imagined perspective of the other party, a third party,
a cultural norm or hypothetical parties

Purpose: To open perspectives and create insight safely.

Underlying Interests Questions
Conflict Triggers, Impact, Beliefs, Values and Attitudes

*Purpose: To move the conflict positions of the parties to the core
of their conflict, and identify needs and underlying interests.*

Future Focus Questions
Hypothetical, Conditional, Consequential,
BATNA / MLATNA / WATNA

*Purpose: To move parties off the conflict treadmill and facilitate
cognitive thinking, leading to options and solutions.*

Figure: 12.1.
CREDIT: O'SULLIVAN SOLUTIONS

S4: Distinction and Difference Questions

DISTINCTION AND DIFFERENCE QUESTIONS bring clarity, relevance, measurement, boundary and a different perspective to conflict issues. Asking questions that explore the distinctions and differences in how parties are thinking, and that create distinctions between the various facets of a conflict, supports them to think incisively.

How Do Distinction and Difference Questions Work?

These questions slice through the information presented by the parties to identify in what way the issues presented, or their component parts, are a problem. They identify the contexts and times when an issue becomes a problem, measure its priority and importance, and identify alternatives to absolutist negative narratives.

> Example:
>
> When one party thinks that their supervisor is bullying them and is *always on their case*, this type of question helps to identify exactly when, where and in what way the supervisor's behavior is impacting. This helps the perspective of both parties. The complainant's accusations become more concise, enabling the supervisor to know the specifics of the accusation, rather than thinking that the complainant thought she was a bully all the time, and in every way imaginable.

When to Ask Distinction and Difference Questions

This type of question is used when parties seem to have become consumed by their conflict, are incapable of breaking down the various elements of their conflict or are unable to think clearly.

These questions are used:

✓ When clarity and focus is needed

✓ When parties struggle to understand what each other is saying

✓ When clarity for the complained against is needed so that the specifics of the complaint are understood, and therefore an appropriate change of behavior can be identified

✓ When measurement is needed regarding something that requires more precise information, e.g., the relevance or importance of something; the extent of an impact on parties; the level of understanding reached; the progress made; the relevance of solutions and the level of satisfaction with agreements; or anything else that requires precise information

✓ When parties are unable to step back from the conflict and view it with an alternative perspective

✓ When a cultural difference, or a difference in values, forms the basis of the conflict

✓ To assess a party's willingness to engage in or remain in mediation

Methodology

Building Distinction and Difference Questions

Distinction and Difference questions have several sub-elements that can be employed as a subject to develop them. The list of sub-elements in this table is far from exhaustive.

Distinction and Difference Questions *Sub-elements*	
▪ Parts	▪ Spatial
▪ People	▪ Comparisons
▪ Contexts/Environment	▪ Time Span
▪ Opposites	▪ Measurement/Ranking

When a party makes a statement, build a Distinction and Difference question by taking these sub-elements and using them to find out more information.

Example:

Ask whether the problem arises with only some **people** and not with other **people**, ask how other people get on with this person (**comparison**), ask if there are different **parts** to the problem and how each part differs from other parts, ask if the **context** makes a difference to the situation. A question can be posed that asks about the **opposite** to what a party says:

Example:

Mediator asks: You say it won't work, what would make it work?

Examples of Distinction and Difference Questions Using Each of the Sub-elements

Creating Distinction and Difference Between Parts

Breaking conflict and conflict perspectives into parts focuses a party's mind on what exactly is the problem for them, and what is not the problem. For example, when parties demonstrate confusion, they often refer to different levels or parts within themselves and you can use this as a reference for asking a question. For example, a party may say something like, "On the one hand ... but on the other hand..."

Example: Exploring the different and distinct **parts** of a conflict

- You mention that you are feeling split over this — what exactly is split? How is it split?
- What is your heart telling you? What is your head telling you?
- When you are unhappy with what's happening in this relationship, which parts of the conflict are more likely to take over your thinking? What brings that part to the fore?
- If the lesser part was solved, how would you feel about the bigger part?
- What small part could you let go of that would not make a huge difference to you, but could make a huge difference to the other party?

Creating Distinction and Difference Between People

These questions allow parties to reflect on specifically who is pertinent to the conflict, to what degree, and in what way.

Example: Exploring a workplace relationship conflict

- How would you describe your relationship with each of the people on the team?
- What are the distinctions and differences you see between these relationships?
- To what degree is each person pertinent to this conflict?
- In what way does the atmosphere in the team depend on which people are in the room?
- What is their relationship like with each other?

Creating Distinction and Difference Between Contexts

Asking questions about different contexts helps the parties to identify the conflict in a more focused way and to view it from different context perspectives.

> Example: Exploring behavior in different contexts
>
> - How does her behavior change in different contexts?
> - In what sort of context would that behavior be acceptable? When might it be unacceptable?
> - If she had said that to you in a private context, how would that have been for you?
> - What are the contexts when this is more manageable for you? Less manageable for you?

Creating Distinction and Difference Using Opposites

Looking at opposites often opens the conflict perspective so that it can then be distilled to specifics.

> Example: Exploring alternative possibilities to a relationship difficulty
>
> - What did you hear from John that was opposite to what you expected to hear?
> - I hear you saying that you are disappointed … what needs to happen for you to feel the opposite of this?
> - What did you intend to happen? What did you not intend to happen?
> - How would it be for you if you viewed this issue in the opposite way to how you view it now?

Creating Distinction and Difference Spatially

These questions flag distinctions and differences in proximity, distance or perspective. They can be used to metaphorically check how something looks from a range of perspectives, for example, from up high, down low, the inside, the outside or upside down. They can measure the distance between X and Y; for example, they can identify the distance a process needs to take before reaching the agreement stage.

Example: Exploring distinct and different perspectives to create insight

- If you were to go right down into this conflict, what might this feel like?

- If you were to move further away from it and look at it from up high, as if you were on a balcony, what might you see? What would that feel like?

- How do you think this looks like from where the other party is situated? And how does it look from where you are situated? What would it look like to each of you if you swapped your exact situations?

- What is needed to bridge the gap between where you are now and where you would like to be?

Creating Distinction and Difference by Making Comparisons

If a mediator asks a party to describe their relationship, their response will be informed by comparing their relationship with something else they know; how this relationship was in the past, how it differs from other relationships or by the expectations they had for it. Making comparisons gives a different context and perspective that allows parties to look at information and distill it in a more focused way.

Example: Making comparisons in a relationship before and after a conflict event

- You say your relationship with your business partner is not good, what was it like before you entered the partnership deal? What had been your expectations?

- How does that compare to how it is now?

- How does it compare to other business partnerships that you know?

- What are the distinction and differences between these two comparisons?

- How would you like it to be in the future, compared to the way it is now?

Creating Distinction and Difference Across a Time Span

Time span questions will support the parties to identify the distinctions and differences related to their issue by asking questions across a span of time. Changes in dynamic and feelings can be identified in relation to this span of time.

> Example: When parties are holding on to their anger with each other
>
> - How do you view your relationship with each other now?
> - Was there a time when you thought differently about the relationship? What was it like then?
> - When did you first feel that it had changed?
> - If this latest event had happened when your relationship with each other was good, what might have been different? How might you have interpreted the event then?
> - Might there be a time when you might both feel differently to the way you feel now?
> - I hear you saying that you are not prepared to forgive right now... is there a time in the future when you might be willing to start a journey of forgiveness?

Creating Distinction and Difference Using Measurement and Ranking

Measurement and ranking questions do exactly what the title suggests; they measure and rank something about which you wish to have more precise information, such as the relevance and importance of various issues; the level of impact of the conflict on the parties; the level of understanding reached between parties; the extent to which the needs and underlying interests of parties are being met; the level of progress being made in a mediation process, or about parties' level of orientation toward reaching an agreement with each other; and the extent to which parties' thinking, feeling and experiencing has changed across a span of time. Asking parties to numerically rank something can stimulate new thinking and perspective.

Bannink[42] offers a practitioner perspective, arguing for an adaptation of the scaling process based on cognitive dissonance theory (covered in Chapter 14). Before asking a numerical ranking question, Bannink says that they need to ask some lead-in questions that will raise some of the positive realities in the relationship. By doing this the party will mark themselves at a higher level on the scale and therefore their cognitive dissonance will be less and they will see resolution as being more attainable. This technique needs to be used with integrity and should not be used to illustrate falsehoods.

Examples:
An example of a good time to ask a ranking question would be after some progress has already been achieved in the mediation. The response given by parties will indicate the level of progress they feel they have achieved:

Measurement and ranking questions measure progress:

- In terms of progress toward resolution of this issue, where are each of you now, on a scale of 0 to 10? With 10 being high. What influenced you to give it this ranking?
- What ranking would you have given your prospect of resolution if I had asked you this question when you first arrived to mediation this morning?
- What ranking do you hope you will be able to give your prospect of resolution within another hour?
- What would each of you have said here that would have created the possibility of this ranking becoming a reality in about an hour?
- What would each of you need to be able to progress further?
- When you both return to work, and if this was working well, what measurement of progress toward resolution would each of you like the other party to give at the end of the first day? After a month?
- What would have happened over that period of a month that would allow both of you to give an increase in your ranking measurement?

Hazard Warning

When you ask a ranking question may influence the type of response a party gives to it. For example, it would not be appropriate to ask parties to rank where they are on the scale of 0 to 10 in terms of reaching resolution directly after they have described their current conflict situation, because they will mark themselves at the lower end of the scale.

Hazard Warning

Before asking measurement and ranking questions, a mediator needs to have a sense of the responses that may be given, because if one party says they would mark the progress made as 6 out of 10 and the other party responds with 0, it may create a sense of threat in both parties.

Key Learning

DISTINCTION AND DIFFERENCE QUESTIONS

Distinction and Difference questions bring clarity, relevance, measurement, boundary and a different perspective to conflict issues. Asking questions that explore the distinctions and differences in how parties are thinking, and that create distinctions between the various facets of a conflict, helps the parties to think incisively.

Distinction and Difference questions have several sub-elements that can be employed as a subject to develop this question. The list of sub-elements worked with in this table is not an exhaustive list.

When a party makes a statement, build a Distinctions and Differences question by taking a sub-element and using it to find out more information.

Distinction and Difference Questions *Sub-elements*	
▪ Parts	▪ Spatial
▪ People	▪ Comparisons
▪ Contexts/Environment	▪ Time Span
▪ Opposites	▪ Measurement/Ranking

Example:

Ask whether the **problem** arises with only some people and not with other people, ask how other **people** get on with this person (**comparison**), ask if there are different **parts** to the problem and how each part differs from other parts, ask if the **context** makes a difference to the situation. A question can be posed that asks about the **opposite** to what a party says:

Example:

Mediator asks, "You say it won't work, what would make it work?"

Hazard Warning

It is important to reiterate here that these questions may need to be tested during the initial separate private meeting or in a private meeting during a joint session, if you have any reason to doubt as to whether the response will be positive or affirming.

S4: The Shift Thinking Dimension of Questions

To uncover new information and insight, either by exploring and focusing thinking or by connecting and expanding thinking, leading to a paradigm shift

Journey of Inference Questions
Interpretations, Assumptions, Conclusions, Beliefs, Actions

Purpose: To identify the link between interpretations and actions. To explore parties' current narratives and to shift perspectives toward a new narrative.

Neuro-linguistic Programming (NLP) Based Questions
Deletions, Distortions, Generalizations

Purpose: To bring clarity; explore subjective realities, explore bias and misinterpretations, and create congruency in communication.

Distinction and Difference Questions
People, Parts, Contexts, Opposites, Spatial, Comparisons, Time Span, Measurement or Ranking

Purpose: To bring clarity, relevance, measurement, boundary and a different perspective to the conflict.

Reflective Connecting Questions
Connecting with patterns and cycles of conflict, both intrapersonal and interpersonal, and in the broader context

Purpose: To raise awareness of negative patterns and cycles of conflict, to deconstruct past unhelpful patterns and to reconstruct new healthy patterns.

Cognitive Elements-based Questions
Knowledge; Opinion and Thinking; Beliefs, Values and Attitudes; Behaviour; Sense of Self/Identity; Environment

Purpose: To explore inner conflicts and inconsistencies between perception and reality, and between the six cognitive elements. To seek a paradigm shift that will restore cognitive consonance.

Other People Questions
Explore an imagined perspective of the other party, a third party, a cultural norm or hypothetical parties

Purpose: To open perspectives and create insight safely.

Underlying Interests Questions
Conflict Triggers, Impact, Beliefs, Values and Attitudes

Purpose: To move the conflict positions of the parties to the core of their conflict, and identify needs and underlying interests.

Future Focus Questions
Hypothetical, Conditional, Consequential,
BATNA / MLATNA / WATNA

Purpose: To move parties off the conflict treadmill and facilitate cognitive thinking, leading to options and solutions.

Figure: 13.1.
CREDIT: O'SULLIVAN SOLUTIONS

S4: Reflective Connecting Questions

MANY OF THE CONFLICTS that present at mediation are a result of parties' ingrained patterns of behavior, which do not always serve the purpose for which they were intended. Reflective Connecting questions explore connections between actions and outcomes, patterns of behavior and cycles of conflict, both interpersonally and in the broader context in which the conflict operates. These questions bring clarity, relevance, understanding and a new perspective to a conflict.

How Do Reflective Connecting Questions Work?

When you make connections and links between various facets of a conflict, you broaden and expand the thinking of both parties. Reflective Connecting questions raise awareness of patterns and cycles of conflict, deconstruct this cycle and then reconstruct a more helpful approach for the parties. These questions allow parties to step back, gain perspective and reflect on alternative options and actions.

> Relationship questions that draw connections between relationships and behavior, feelings, beliefs and meanings can create significant new understanding, and thus provide the impetus for change.
>
> — Jac Brown,[44] Director of the Australian Institute for Relationship Studies

When to Ask Reflective Connecting Questions

These questions are used:

✓ When parties are blaming each other without being able to see how their own behavior impacts the continuation of this conflict cycle

✓ When parties display patterns or cycles of negative behavior with each other; when the actions of one party sparks the actions of the other, leading to an intensification of the cycle

✓ When parties do not see the link between their actions and resulting outcomes and continue to employ the same behavior, expecting different results

✓ When a party is unaware that their actions do not operate in a vacuum, but can impact the broader system

Methodology

Building Reflective Connecting Questions

Reflective Connecting questions are constructed by taking any part of the conflict being discussed and asking questions about how one aspect of the conflict connects with another.

Simply ask: How does X connect with Y?

The steps for working with patterns or cycles of conflict are:

1. Raise awareness about the pattern or cycle of conflict by bringing attention to it
2. Reflect on the patterns or cycles of conflict
3. Create insight and deconstruct the patterns or cycles of conflict
4. Reconstruct healthy patterns and agree on actions

Case study to illustrate examples of Reflective Connecting questions

TWO MANAGERS IN A CYCLE OF CONFLICT

Jack is Irish and has been a manager in a café in Dublin since it opened 15 years ago. Ivan is Polish and was promoted as manager a year ago. Ivan had started work in the café only two years prior to this, but the owner of the café had seen his managerial potential immediately and asked him to manage the café for the evening shift, while Jack continued to manage the day shift.

Tensions arose in the first weeks when the owner had, on several occasions, publicly commended Ivan on his excellent professionalism as a manager. Jack felt threatened by this and started to resent Ivan. When Jack arrived to do his day shift, he began to openly criticize Ivan's work from the previous evening. After a few weeks, Ivan started to complain about Jack's work when he arrived for the evening shift, as he felt he had to do something to protect his reputation. Most of the evening staff were Polish, while most of the day staff were Irish, and they each began to take sides with the manager who was the same nationality as themselves.

At the start, Ivan was not happy criticizing Jack's work, but as things became worse, he felt quite justified in doing so as a pattern of complaint and counter-complaint had become normal, everyday practice between them. The owner of the café began to see that this conflict was affecting all the staff, so he offered a mediation process to the two managers, to which they agreed.

Reflective Connecting questions will target two facets of this conflict:

1. The interpersonal cycles of conflict
2. The broader system to which the conflict connects

1. Interpersonal Cycles of Conflict

Where a spiral of conflict has developed and the actions of each party are influenced by the actions or reactions of the other party, then a pattern develops that creates a continuation of the conflict cycle. Each party starts to blame the other party for everything that happens and says that they would not have taken this action if the other person had not done something to them first.

Examples of questions:

a) Raise awareness about the pattern or cycle of conflict by bringing attention to it

   Mediator asks:

   > Both of you say that every day there is a new complaint from one of you about the other, but that this conflict is the fault of the other. May I ask you both some questions about this pattern or cycle that may have developed between you, please?

b) Reflect on the patterns or cycles of conflict

   - When one of you makes a complaint about the other, what happens next? And then what happens? In what way do each of your responses determine what the other party does next?
   - And how does this connect with what happens next?
   - How does what each of you does affect (i) the direction of the conflict, (ii) its continuation, (iii) its intensification?

c) Create insight by deconstructing the patterns or cycles of conflict

   - What are you trying to achieve when you make a complaint about the other? How does the outcome connect with what you really need? How helpful/unhelpful might this be for both of you?
   - How does this impact on each of you? Can you both tell me a little more about what each of you may be worried about should the conflict continue?
   - If you were each to imagine you were on a balcony looking down at what happens between you, what might you observe?
   - What are the commonalities in the way you each approach this and react? What are the differences? What might be the pattern that may have developed between the two of you?
   - How does the approach you use with each other compare to your usual approach when you are in conflict?
   - What is the connection between what you are doing and your beliefs about how people manage conflict?

d) Reconstruct healthy patterns and agree on actions

- If you were to reflect on all you have both just said, what might be your conclusion?
- What would happen if you broke the connection between what each of you does and how the other reacts? What would that give you?
- What would happen if you connected with a different response, what outcomes might result?
- What do each of you need to do to break the connection between what one of you does and how the other party responds?
- How would that connect with what you both say you really need?
- If this was to work well, how would each of you describe it? What would it look like to each of you? What could you offer to each other to ensure it looks like this?
- What will you do if you see yourself lapsing into a pattern like this again?
- What might you decide to do from now on? How will you manage it so that it works for you?

2. The Broader System in Which the Conflict Exists

These questions facilitate parties to see how their conflict connects, not only with their patterns of behavior or the conflict cycle that has developed between them, but also with the broader environment in which they work. They help parties to see that their conflict does not occur in a vacuum and that their continuation of the conflict, or indeed their resolution of the conflict, will have an impact on the rest of staff.

Examples of questions:

a) Raise awareness about the pattern or cycle of conflict by bringing attention to it

Mediator asks:

Ivan and Jack, you mention that this conflict between you has gone on for many months now... and that the staff are aware of what is happening between you... and that they have broken into two factions, with each side mainly supporting their own manager ...

b) Reflect on the patterns and cycles of conflict

- What might staff say about the general atmosphere in the café?
- What do you think the staff see during these incidences?
- What connections might staff notice about how you respond to each other?

c) Create insight and deconstruct the patterns or cycles of conflict

- How do you think staff interpret what is happening? What assumptions might they make? What might they conclude? What do they do then?
- How does the behavior that you two engage in with each other connect with how members of staff behave with each other?
- What do you think staff may be most concerned about? What might be their biggest concern?
- How does this conflict impact on them?
- How does this conflict impact on the business? What could be the long-term damage?

d) Reconstruct healthy patterns and decide action

- What might staff need from each of you? What could you both agree to offer them?
- What will each of you do if a member of staff comes to you and blames the other manager for something that has happened?
- If something like this happens between you two again, how will each of you manage it? What could you promise to each other?
- What do you need to communicate to staff after this mediation? How will this be done?
- What if staff ask each of you privately about what happened in mediation, what response could you agree to give them?

Key Learning

REFLECTIVE CONNECTING QUESTIONS

Reflective Connecting questions broaden and expand the thinking of the parties. They are constructed by taking any part of the conflict being discussed and asking questions about how one aspect of the conflict connects with another.

Simply ask: How does X connect with Y?

Reflective Connecting questions can be used to explore:

1. Interpersonal cycles of conflict

2. The broader system in which the conflict exists

The steps to take when working with patterns or cycles of conflict are:

a) Raise awareness about the pattern or cycle of conflict by bringing attention to it

b) Reflect on the patterns or cycles of conflict

c) Create insight and deconstruct the patterns or cycles of conflict

d) Reconstruct healthy patterns and agree actions

Hazard Warning

Do not pressure a party to answer a question — proceed carefully and gently, at their pace, and with their permission. Should you inadvertently touch on any past trauma of a party, then slowly and gently name the fact that you have touched on it, acknowledge that it must have caused deep pain, and then ask what needs to be in place for the future.

14

S4: The Shift Thinking Dimension of Questions

To uncover new information and insight, either by exploring and focusing thinking
or by connecting and expanding thinking, leading to a paradigm shift

Journey of Inference Questions
Interpretations, Assumptions, Conclusions, Beliefs, Actions

*Purpose: To identify the link between interpretations and actions.
To explore parties' current narratives and to shift perspectives
toward a new narrative.*

Neuro-linguistic Programming (NLP) Based Questions
Deletions, Distortions, Generalizations

*Purpose: To bring clarity; explore subjective realities,
explore bias and misinterpretations, and create congruency
in communication.*

Distinction and Difference Questions
People, Parts, Contexts, Opposites, Spatial, Comparisons,
Time Span, Measurement or Ranking

*Purpose: To bring clarity, relevance, measurement, boundary
and a different perspective to the conflict.*

Reflective Connecting Questions
Connecting with patterns and cycles of conflict, both
intrapersonal and interpersonal, and in the broader context

*Purpose: To raise awareness of negative patterns and
cycles of conflict, to deconstruct past unhelpful patterns
and to reconstruct new healthy patterns.*

Cognitive Elements-based Questions
Knowledge; Opinion and Thinking; Beliefs, Values and Attitudes;
Behaviour; Sense of Self/Identity; Environment

*Purpose: To explore inner conflicts and inconsistencies between
perception and reality, and between the six cognitive elements.
To seek a paradigm shift that will restore cognitive consonance.*

Other People Questions
Explore an imagined perspective of the other party, a third party,
a cultural norm or hypothetical parties

Purpose: To open perspectives and create insight safely.

Underlying Interests Questions
Conflict Triggers, Impact, Beliefs, Values and Attitudes

*Purpose: To move the conflict positions of the parties to the core
of their conflict, and identify needs and underlying interests.*

Future Focus Questions
Hypothetical, Conditional, Consequential,
BATNA / MLATNA / WATNA

*Purpose: To move parties off the conflict treadmill and facilitate
cognitive thinking, leading to options and solutions.*

Figure: 14.1.

S4: Cognitive Elements Questions

COGNITIVE ELEMENTS-BASED QUESTIONS explore inconsistencies (cognitive dissonance) between our cognitive elements, which are: our knowledge; our opinions and thinking; our beliefs, values and attitudes; our behaviors; our sense of self or identity; and our environment. These questions explore the psychological conflicts that result when one or more of our cognitive elements are in dissonance with another cognitive element, simultaneously.

Example of cognitive dissonance:

When I know (cognitive element: knowledge) that smoking is damaging to my health, but I continue to smoke anyway (cognitive element: behavior).

Chapter 3 illustrated how biological hardwiring, governed by memories of stimuli, activates an avoid-threat reflex in us. Our life experience demonstrates to us that when we react with an avoid-threat reflex, we are correct to do so, as it reduces the sense of threat that we experience. But when this correctness is shaken or challenged, it creates uncertainty in us and we enter into a state of cognitive dissonance.

Before moving to the methodology of developing Cognitive Elements-based questions, it is important to look at some background theory first, including the definition of cognitive dissonance and an explanation of each of the cognitive elements.

Theoretical Background

The theory of cognitive dissonance was developed by Leon Festinger [43] in 1957. He defined it as a psychological conflict which results when one of our cognitive elements is incongruent with another element, simultaneously.

Definition of Cognition

Cognition is any knowledge, opinion or belief that we have about our sense of self or identity, or our behavior, or our environment.

Cognitive Dissonance and Cognitive Consonance

Cognitive dissonance and cognitive consonance refer to relations that exist, simultaneously, between any pair of elements of cognition, such as between our beliefs and what we experience in our environment; between our knowledge and our beliefs; or between our opinion of ourselves and our actual behavior.

For cognitive dissonance to exist within a person, there needs to be a relation between a pair of cognitive elements.

Example of a relation between the cognitive elements of belief and behavior:

If we have a very strong belief about equality between the sexes, but we also value making a profit, then we may experience dissonance between our belief in the equality of the sexes and our behavior of strategically hiring an older woman because she will not need maternity leave and will therefore be less costly to us. In this instance, our beliefs, values and attitudes and our behaviors have a relation with each other and are in dissonance with each other, simultaneously. When two or more cognitive elements are incongruent with each other, we experience dissonance, are thrown out of balance and then strive to return to harmony and cognitive consonance.

Cognitive consonance occurs:

a) When there is no relation between a pair of cognitive elements.

Example:

Beliefs, values or attitudes: I believe that the world is round.

Behavior: I bought an ice cream today.

b) When there is a relation between a pair of elements, but they are congruent with each other, simultaneously.

> Example:
>
> Beliefs, values or attitudes: I believe it is very important to take care of those who are elderly and living alone.
>
> Behavior: My elderly neighbor lives alone, and I call to visit her daily.

Festinger's theory focuses on how people strive for internal consistency and balance. When they experience inconsistency (dissonance between the elements of cognition), individuals tend to become psychologically uncomfortable and are motivated to attempt to reduce this dissonance, as well as to actively avoid situations and information that are likely to increase it. Festinger suggests that we are driven to hold all our attitudes and beliefs in harmony (consonance), and to avoid disharmony (dissonance).

Festinger's Hypotheses

Festinger worked from two basic hypotheses:

- That the existence of dissonance, being psychologically uncomfortable, will motivate a person to try to reduce that dissonance and achieve consonance.
- That when dissonance is present, as well as trying to reduce it, a person will actively avoid situations and information that would be likely to increase the dissonance.

The Framework of Cognitive Elements

Cognitive Elements
Festinger describes our six cognitive elements as being; our behaviour; our beliefs, values and attitudes; our opinion and thinking; our knowledge; our sense of self or identity and our environment.

Definition of Cognition:
Any knowledge, opinion or belief that we have about our sense of self or identity or our behaviour or the environment (the physical, social and psychological world in which we live).

Cognitive Dissonance Theory:
This is defined as a psychological conflict that results when one of our cognitive elements is incongruent with another one, simultaneously.

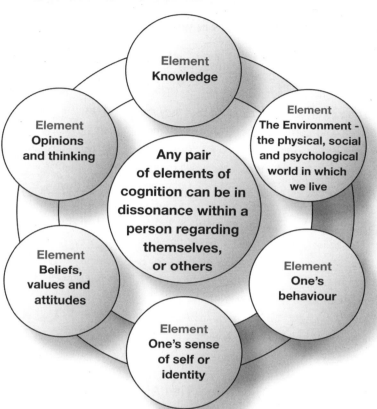

The Six Cognitive Elements

Knowledge
The process of knowing, including aspects such as thinking, learning, awareness, reasoning, judgment, perception, intuition, understanding.

Opinions/Thinking
How we view the world, judgment, or appraisal formed in the mind about a particular matter considered to be subjective.

The Environment
The physical, social and psychological world/context in which we live. What is where? What leads to what? What is satisfying, painful, inconsequential, etc?

Beliefs, Values, Attitudes
A belief is an internal feeling that something is true, even though that belief may be unproven or irrational. A value is a measure of the worth or importance we attach to something; An attitude is the way we express or apply our beliefs and values.

One's Behaviour
What I do and how I behave, my actions and reactions.

One's Sense of Self or Identity
Our sense of self or identity, our interests, feelings, needs, desires etc.

Figure: 14.2.

Case study to illustrate the theory of cognitive dissonance

THE GRADUAL CHANGING OF BELIEFS IN WARRING FACTIONS, LEADING TO A CHANGE OF BEHAVIOR

How often do the people on one side of a major conflict believe that the people on the other side are bad, evil or terrorists? They believe that there is not one good person on the other side and that they are all dangerous and carry guns, and that even their children carry knives in their school bags. They state that everyone on the other side wants to kill them.

It is only by employing this level of belief that they can reconcile their behavior of shooting, torturing and imprisoning people from the other side, including children. This belief helps them to remain in cognitive consonance. They also believe that their behavior is justified and that they have to do it to defend themselves because of what happened in the past.

At political peace negotiations, the beliefs that each side have of the other side start to change as they get to listen to and experience each other. They begin to realize that some of the people with whom they are negotiating are human. This can cause increased cognitive dissonance for them. If one of them has had a brother shot dead by the other side, they will start to cope with this dissonance by saying to themselves — this guy seems fine, but the rest of them are all terrorists. But during successful peace negotiations, this dialogue and sharing will start to shift their thinking, very slowly. This can be the powerful result of having a mediation/negotiation process where parties increasingly meet jointly as the process progresses.

The Factors That Affect Cognitive Dissonance and Cognitive Consonance

Before moving to the methodology to use when asking Cognitive Elements-based questions, we need to first look at the following:

1. Determinants of the presence of cognitive dissonance
2. Magnitude of cognitive dissonance
3. Blocks to reducing cognitive dissonance
4. The strategies we may use to defend against experiencing cognitive dissonance
5. Post-decision cognitive consonance

1. DETERMINANTS OF THE PRESENCE OF COGNITIVE DISSONANCE

The amount of cognitive dissonance in parties will fluctuate throughout the course of a mediation, and will be dependent on:

- Whether the type of question that is asked of a party results in any feelings of threat;
- Whether one party says something that will affect the cognitive consonance of the other party;
- Whether the parties start to understand each other, or not, as a result of increased knowledge;
- Whether the parties start to problem-solve together as a result of attitudinal change;
- Whether one party makes a positive gesture to the other;
- Whether the parties have made any positive agreements with each other around future behavior; etc.

2. MAGNITUDE OF COGNITIVE DISSONANCE

The magnitude of cognitive dissonance we experience is related to:

- The degree to which any cognitive element is inconsistent with another cognitive element;
- How important we consider the conflicting cognitive elements to be;
- How highly we value a specific cognitive element.

When we experience cognitive dissonance, we strive to reduce or eliminate this dissonance or threat. The strength of the pressure needed to reduce the dissonance is related to the magnitude of the dissonance. As the magnitude increases, the pressure to reduce dissonance increases. The maximum dissonance that can possibly exist for a person is equal to the total resistance to change of the less resistant element.

Case study to illustrate the increase in magnitude of cognitive dissonance

TRYING TO STOP SMOKING

Take the example of the cognitive dissonance that arises between the knowledge and behavior of a person who smokes cigarettes. If David has smoked for many years, then he has probably been able to manage the level of dissonance between his cognitive knowledge (he knows it's bad for his health) and his cognitive element of behavior (he keeps on smoking anyway).

But if David begins to experience signs that his smoking behavior is having a serious effect on him, such as noticing the wheeze in his breathing or being told by his doctor that his heart has being affected, then David's knowledge will increase, and so will the magnitude of the dissonance he experiences. This could result in the dissonance becoming greater than his resistance to stop smoking, and therefore he will stop smoking.

3. BLOCKS TO REDUCING COGNITIVE DISSONANCE

There are several reasons why we may find it difficult to change elements of cognition so that we achieve cognitive consonance:

- The change may be painful or may involve loss

  Example:

  I have a good social life with friends and I really enjoy their company, but if I want to stop smoking then I will have to avoid all social occasions for a while so I am not tempted to smoke.

- The decision that resulted in cognitive dissonance may be difficult to revoke

  Example:

  If I regret selling my home last year, then I cannot un-sell it.

- If changing one of the elements results in cognitive dissonance with another element

  Example:

  If my employer says that I should not wear a hijab, and if my religious beliefs or culture advocate that I must wear a hijab, then I will experience dissonance if I obey my employer. If I try to reduce this dissonance by leaving my job as a legal intern, then I will create cognitive dissonance between my cognitive element of behavior in leaving and my cognitive elements of beliefs, values and attitudes, as I believe that the best way that I can become a good lawyer and defend human rights abuses is by staying with this company.

4. THE STRATEGIES WE MAY USE TO DEFEND AGAINST EXPERIENCING COGNITIVE DISSONANCE

When observable data contradict our interpretations, assumptions, conclusions and beliefs, we experience cognitive dissonance. This could happen to a party that we take through a series of S4: Journey of Inference questions. They will then seek to achieve cognitive consonance as quickly as possible to regain their comfort about what is happening to them. If dissonance is not reduced by changing one of the cognitive elements, a party may restore consonance through misperception, blaming others, rejecting the information they are faced with, attempting to persuade others to understand their point of view or by seeking support from others who share their beliefs.

We create our falsehoods by filtering information and deleting, distorting and generalizing the information that we absorb, as evidenced in Chapter 11. Over a lifetime, we develop a range of tools and skills for reducing cognitive dissonance when we are conflicted.

Note:

CE: Cognitive Element

Example:

We justify smoking cigarettes by saying:

> There is a far higher chance that I will be killed by a car, than by the few cigarettes that I smoke.

Case study to illustrate the way we defend against experiencing cognitive dissonance

A COMPANY CHIEF EXECUTIVE ACCUSED BY A SENIOR MANAGER OF BULLYING BEHAVIOR

Take the example of the cognitive dissonance that may arise for the CEO of a company who is accused of bullying behavior (CE: behavior) by a senior manager. The CEO has a belief (CE: belief) that if senior managers are not controlled and micromanaged, then they will not produce the work standards that are required. He believes that the authoritarian way of working is the only way to achieve success. But even though the CEO strongly states that he can defend the bullying complaint from his senior manager easily, he feels a little uneasy about it and starts to experience some cognitive dissonance. To deal with this, he decides to ask some like-minded colleagues how they behave with staff to achieve productivity, but he introduces his question by saying that he is having a problem with a lazy employee. Referring to his employee as lazy will ensure that the responses he receives match his current behavior and that he will not be in cognitive dissonance.

Meanwhile, at home, the CEO's nine-year-old daughter is telling him (CE: knowledge) that she is having problems with her teacher. She says her teacher shouts at her and bullies her all the time. She has even come home from school in tears some days. So now as the CEO reflects on the bullying complaint against him, he begins to experience a little bit more cognitive dissonance. How is he going to manage it?

To achieve cognitive consonance, the CEO may employ any of the following strategies to either eliminate or reduce this cognitive dissonance:

a) He could change one of his original conflicting cognitive elements of belief or behavior.

b) He could change the level of importance of one of his cognitive elements.

c) He could add a new cognition to one of the conflicting elements of belief or behavior.

d) He could make a decision that will achieve cognitive consonance later.

    a) He could **change one of the conflicting elements** of belief or behavior:

- He could strengthen his original cognitive element of **belief** that excessive micromanagement is necessary for high productivity and then his cognitive element of **behavior** would change.

or

- He could learn (CE: knowledge) from his colleagues that pressurizing employees only makes matters worse as employees becomes stressed by it and cannot function effectively and work productively. Therefore, he will change his cognitive element of **behavior.**

    b) He could **reduce or decrease the importance of one of the conflicting elements** of belief or behavior by changing his perception of his behavior or his belief:

- He could continue the bullying **behavior** by completely denying to himself that his **behavior** causes any harm to his manager cognitive elements of belief.

or

- He could strengthen his **belief** that the whole system will fall apart and productivity will go down drastically if he lessens control over his manager. Therefore, his behavior will match his belief.

c) He could **add a new cognition** to one of the conflicting elements of belief or behavior:

- He could add a new cognition to his **behavior** and decide to only criticize the manager in private because his daughter told him that being bullied in front of others in the classroom was the worst part of her experience.

or

- He could add a new cognition to his **belief** that persuades him that adults and children are not the same:
  She is only a child, but my manager will just have to toughen up, really.

d) He could make decisions (behaviors) that may **achieve cognitive consonance later**:

- If the existing cognitions cannot be changed, and a new cognition cannot be added now, then behaviors that may favor consonance in the future might be agreed. The CEO could decide to participate in a management training course to learn what the industry norms are regarding the link between management style and productivity.

5. POST-DECISION COGNITIVE CONSONANCE

If the CEO decides to change either his cognitive element of belief or his cognitive element of behavior, or to not change any of his cognitive elements, he will then only absorb information that confirms this belief or behavior he has chosen and will avoid any contradictory information so that he remains in cognitive consonance.

Once parties have made decisions and reached agreement in mediation, after reality testing, and when they have successfully achieved cognitive consonance, it is difficult for them to change their minds, as this may increase cognitive dissonance for them again. This is particularly important to note with regard to the mediated agreements that the clients of mediators agree and sign.

Once people have made a decision, they usually start to reduce any post-decision dissonance in the following ways:

a) By decreasing the attractiveness of the options that they did *not* choose, and by seeking more positive information about the options that they *did* choose. This proves to them that they have made the correct decision.

b) By perceiving that some of the characteristics of the options they have chosen are the same as some of the characteristics of the options they did not choose, thus reducing the dissonance.

c) By increasing or decreasing the importance of various aspects of the options chosen, in line with the decisions that they made.

Case study: seeking post-decision cognitive consonance

STRIVING TO MAINTAIN COGNITIVE CONSONANCE CAN LEAD TO MALADAPTIVE BEHAVIOR

Leon Festinger states that once we make decisions, we try to reduce or eliminate our internal cognitive dissonance, even if this results in us behaving in an irrational or maladaptive manner.

For example, Festinger first investigated cognitive dissonance out of a participant observation study of a cult that believed that the Earth was going to be destroyed by a flood. He looked at how the cult members reacted when their prediction of the end of the world did not transpire. Specifically, he looked at the reactions of the strongly committed members who had given up their homes and jobs to work for the cult.

While fringe members were more inclined to recognize that they had made fools of themselves, committed members were more likely to reinterpret the evidence to show that they had been right all along, and that the Earth was not destroyed because of their faith and prayers. If they did not reinterpret the evidence this way, it would have resulted in increased cognitive dissonance for them, as they had given up so much to work for the cult. So they maintained cognitive consonance by ensuring that their cognitive element of belief remained in harmony with their cognitive element of behavior. In conclusion, they adapted their cognitive element of belief in order to remain in cognitive consonance.

How Do Cognitive Elements-based Questions Work?

If parties are already experiencing cognitive dissonance, or if a mediator decides to strategically work to produce cognitive dissonance in a party, then the party will tend to become psychologically uncomfortable and will be motivated to attempt to reduce this dissonance and disharmony and return to harmony and cognitive consonance.

Cognitive Elements-based questions bring any inconsistencies between a party's cognitive elements to a conscious level and challenges that perspective and paradigm. A mediator can work with this dissonance and facilitate a party to explore the cognitive elements that are in dissonance so that they can get to the root of their inner conflict, and then facilitate them to identify the appropriate changes that will result in them achieving cognitive consonance and harmony again.

When to Ask Cognitive Elements-based Questions

Cognitive Elements-based questions are used:

✓ When it is unclear what motivates or guides a party's approach or behaviors
✓ When inner conflict or disharmony may exist within a party
✓ When a party is unable to progress to reaching agreement
✓ When a party is strongly defending their position and this conflict perspective is inhibiting movement toward a solution
✓ When the stated or apparent impact on a party seems greater than that which would have been expected under any given circumstance
✓ To facilitate the parties to make connections with their cognitive elements so that their perspective is expanded
✓ When a mediator needs to strategically challenge one of the cognitive elements (e.g., behavior or beliefs) of a party because that party's current behavior is impacting negatively on the conflict dynamic

Methodology

Guidelines for Asking a Series of Questions Related to Cognitive Elements

Chapter 4 contains generic guidelines for asking questions, but there are additional specific guidelines for asking Cognitive Elements-based questions.

In asking Cognitive Elements-based questions, it is very important to not expose any vulnerability of one party in front of the other party. If you think that a party may be vulnerable, test out any Cognitive Elements-based questions, either at the initial separate private meeting or during a private meeting during the joint session.

✓ It is important to ensure that a party has told their story and has had an opportunity to vent their emotions about their situation before asking challenging Cognitive Elements-based questions.

✓ Ensure that questions are delivered in a nonjudgmental way, with gentle, open and respectful body language, as a party may easily become defensive, particularly if they have low self-esteem.

✓ Do not pressure a party to answer a question — proceed carefully and gently, at their pace, and with their permission. Should you inadvertently touch on any past trauma of a party, then slowly and gently name the fact that you have touched on it, acknowledge that it must have caused deep pain, and then ask what needs to be in place to address their conflict issues for the future.

✓ When cognitive dissonance has been created, the mediator needs to ensure that the parties will be brought to cognitive consonance with whatever decisions are made. This is where the role of reality testing the mediation agreements is very important.

Working with Cognitive Elements

We can work with Cognitive Elements-based questions in two ways:

1. To proactively trigger cognitive dissonance
2. When a party displays cognitive dissonance

1. Using Cognitive Elements-based Questions to Proactively Trigger Cognitive Dissonance

There may be times when a mediator needs to strategically choose to trigger cognitive dissonance and a negative emotional response from parties. This needs to be done using respectful and gentle body language.

> For example, when a party states one thing, but their actions contradict it:
>
> > It often happens that separating couples engage in mediation and state loudly and forcefully that the most important thing to them is the welfare of their children. Then they start to metaphorically kill each other and try to block the other parent from spending time with their children.
>
> Mediator proactively triggers cognitive dissonance:
>
> > I have observed that you both say very clearly that the most important thing to you is the welfare of your children. I have also observed that you are both finding great difficulty in meeting the needs of your children if it means that one of you needs to give something to the other. What might be going on for each of you when you are like this? Can you help me understand?

2. Using Cognitive Elements-based Questions When a Party Displays Cognitive Dissonance

Cognitive Elements-based questions can also be asked of a party who has either displayed or expressed inner uncomfortableness or contradiction.

In both of the above circumstances, questions are introduced that raise the premise that one or more elements of cognition within a party may not be harmonious with another element. The questions asked need to first build and hold cognitive dissonance in the parties. Then the motivation within the parties to reduce this dissonance and to achieve cognitive consonance will increase. Having worked with, or created, dissonance, the mediator then needs to work with the party to restore cognitive consonance or harmony. The challenge for a mediator is to ensure that cognitive consonance is reached in a helpful way for both parties.

Note:

Prior to actively choosing to trigger cognitive dissonance and an emotional reaction, the mediator needs to know exactly what they want to achieve by asking a question that could result in a negative response from the party, and why they need to do this. It is also important to ensure that none of the questions asked create a vulnerable or unsafe place for either or both parties.

Building Cognitive Elements-based Questions

Step 1: Bring attention to the cognitive dissonance

Step 2: Build and hold cognitive dissonance

Step 3: Reduce cognitive dissonance and work toward cognitive consonance by facilitating the party to:

a) Change one of his original conflicting cognitive elements of belief or behavior

b) Change the level of importance of one of his cognitive elements

c) Add a new cognition to one of the conflicting elements of belief or behavior

d) Make a decision that achieves cognitive consonance later

Step 4: Support the party to look at options and reach solutions for the conflict that will achieve cognitive consonance and be in the best interests of both parties.

Case study to demonstrate the asking of Cognitive Elements-based questions

BUSINESS OWNER AND MANAGER — PROFESSIONAL RELATIONSHIP DURING A FINANCIAL RECESSION

Rebecca is the owner of a medium-sized company where Sarah has been a senior manager for more than twenty years. The company is not doing well because of the recession and the downturn in the economy. Rebecca needed to make changes, including making a junior manager redundant, so she asked Sarah to take additional responsibility for that junior manager's position. Sarah was not happy with this and demonstrated her anger to Rebecca and stormed out of her office.

The mediator is now having a private meeting with Rebecca, asking her how she felt after Sarah was angry with her and what had this display of anger engendered in her? When Rebecca had vented her own frustration at the way Sarah had shouted at her, she then spoke about how she, Rebecca, was not comfortable about the decision she had made to give Sarah more responsibility because it clashed with her beliefs and values about fairness. The mediator then started to ask Cognitive Elements-based questions.

Questions for Building, Holding and Reducing Cognitive Dissonance
(CE: cognitive element)

STEP 1: BRING ATTENTION TO THE COGNITIVE DISSONANCE

Mediator reflecting back:

- Rebecca, you mention that you are a strong believer in fairness and that you always did everything to ensure you were fair to your staff. You mention that because the recession has impacted your business greatly, you are now doing things that you would not have considered fair before the recession — will you tell me more about this?

STEP 2: BUILD AND HOLD COGNITIVE DISSONANCE

These questions create and build dissonance:

- How is it for you when your actions (CE: behavior) contradict what you think is right (CE: beliefs, values and attitudes)?
- What is it like for you to be in this conflict now with Sarah, who you say you value highly?
- What are all the questions that you may have been asking yourself about this? What is it like for you to be in this dilemma?
- How might Sarah be feeling about all this?
- What might happen if this is not sorted?

STEP 3: REDUCE COGNITIVE DISSONANCE AND WORK TOWARD COGNITIVE CONSONANCE

Cognitive dissonance can be reduced by using one of the following methods.

a) Party could change one of the original conflicting cognitions (e.g., belief or behavior)

Change in beliefs and values:

- Giving marks out of 10, how important is it for you to hold onto this belief or value?
  10 = very important and 0 = no importance. What gives it this importance for you?
- Given the circumstances of the recession, how fair are you being toward yourself in trying to uphold your belief in fairness? Marks out of 10?
- What might set your mind at ease about it?

Change in behavior:

- What did you hope to achieve with this action (CE: behavior)?
- How is it meeting your beliefs and values? How is it not meeting them?
- What are all your options around changing your actions (CE: behavior)?
- How might a business colleague put your actions (CE: behavior) into context? What might they advise you? How would you advise yourself?

In conclusion, what are all the options that are open to you so that your belief around fairness and your actions are compatible with each other? With what options might you be more comfortable?

b) Change the level of importance of one of the cognitions

- How important is it for you to continue with this belief in this context? 0 = not important, 10 = very important.
- How important is it for you to continue with this action that you needed to take in this context? 0 = not important, 10 = very important.
- What does this tell you?
- What might help you to reduce/increase the importance of your belief so that you are more comfortable with your actions (CE: behavior)? How could this be managed?
- What might help you to reduce/increase the importance of your action so that you are more comfortable with your beliefs? How could this be managed?

c) Add a new cognition to one of the conflicting elements of belief or behavior

- What might happen if you were to change how you thought (CE: opinions and thinking) about all this?
- What information (CE: knowledge) is out there that could help you to modify your belief in fairness in some way?
- Is there any new information (CE: knowledge) to be gained that could change your views of your action?
- Is there another belief (CE: belief) that could override your belief in fairness?

- What is this conflict between your beliefs and your behavior doing to your sense of yourself (CE: sense of self/identity)? How would you rate the importance to you of each of these cognitive elements: beliefs and values; behavior; sense of self/identity; opinions and thinking? What does this say to you?

d) Make a decision that achieves cognitive consonance later

- Is there a period of time during which you would be prepared to modify your belief until the recession ends?

- What would happen if you put an end date on your actions and requests of Sarah and informed her of this end date?

STEP 4: LOOKING AT OPTIONS AND ACHIEVING COGNITIVE CONSONANCE

- What are all your options?
- What would each of your options give you? Not give you?
- Which option would help to settle the inner conflict that you talked about?
- What would it be like for both of you if this was achieved?

Linking Cognitive Elements-based Questions with Other S4 Questions

- S4: Journey of Inference questions challenge interpretations and assumptions and can be used in exploring or creating cognitive dissonance.
- S4: NLP-based questions around the area of distortion help parties to think about their thinking.
- S4: Underlying Interests questions are helpful in exploring the cognitive elements of beliefs, values and attitudes. Chapter 16 includes options on what a mediator can do if they reach an impasse when working with a party's values.

Key Learning

Cognitive Elements-based questions explore inconsistencies (cognitive dissonance) between our cognitive elements, namely our knowledge; our opinions and thinking; our beliefs, values and attitudes; our behaviors; our sense of self or identity; and our environment. These questions explore the psychological conflicts that result when one or more of our cognitive elements are in dissonance with another cognitive element, simultaneously.

Definition of Cognition:

Any knowledge, opinion or belief that we have about our sense of self or identity, or our behavior, or our environment.

Cognitive Dissonance and Cognitive Consonance

These terms refer to relations that exist, simultaneously, between any pair of elements of cognition, such as between our beliefs and what we experience in our environment; between our knowledge and our beliefs; and between our opinion of ourselves and our behavior.

Cognitive Dissonance:

For cognitive dissonance to exist within a person, there needs to be a relation between a pair of cognitive elements.

Cognitive Consonance:

Cognitive consonance occurs (a) when our cognitive elements have no relation between them or (b) when they have a relation, and are congruent with each other, simultaneously.

Building Cognitive Elements-based questions

Step 1: Bring attention to the cognitive dissonance

Step 2: Build and hold cognitive dissonance

Step 3: Reduce cognitive dissonance and work toward cognitive consonance

This can be done in a number of ways:

a) Change one of his original conflicting cognitive elements of belief or behavior

b) Change the level of importance of one of his cognitive elements

c) Add a new cognition to one of the conflicting elements of belief or behavior

d) Make a decision that achieves cognitive consonance later

Step 4: Look at options and reach solutions for the conflict that will achieve cognitive consonance and be in the best interests of both parties

---

Hazard Warning

It is important to reiterate here that these questions may need to be tested during the initial separate private meeting or in a private meeting during a joint session.

Hazard Warning

Do not pressure a party to answer a question — proceed carefully and gently, at their pace, and with their permission.

15

S4: The Shift Thinking Dimension of Questions — Other People Questions

S4: The Shift Thinking Dimension of Questions

To uncover new information and insight, either by exploring and focusing thinking or by connecting and expanding thinking, leading to a paradigm shift

Journey of Inference Questions
Interpretations, Assumptions, Conclusions, Beliefs, Actions

Purpose: To identify the link between interpretations and actions. To explore parties' current narratives and to shift perspectives toward a new narrative.

Neuro-linguistic Programming (NLP) Based Questions
Deletions, Distortions, Generalizations

Purpose: To bring clarity; explore subjective realities, explore bias and misinterpretations, and create congruency in communication.

Distinction and Difference Questions
People, Parts, Contexts, Opposites, Spatial, Comparisons, Time Span, Measurement or Ranking

Purpose: To bring clarity, relevance, measurement, boundary and a different perspective to the conflict.

Reflective Connecting Questions
Connecting with patterns and cycles of conflict, both intrapersonal and interpersonal, and in the broader context

Purpose: To raise awareness of negative patterns and cycles of conflict, to deconstruct past unhelpful patterns and to reconstruct new healthy patterns.

Cognitive Elements-based Questions
Knowledge; Opinion and Thinking; Beliefs, Values and Attitudes; Behaviour; Sense of Self/Identity; Environment

Purpose: To explore inner conflicts and inconsistencies between perception and reality, and between the six cognitive elements. To seek a paradigm shift that will restore cognitive consonance.

Other People Questions
Explore an imagined perspective of the other party, a third party, a cultural norm or hypothetical parties

Purpose: To open perspectives and create insight safely.

Underlying Interests Questions
Conflict Triggers, Impact, Beliefs, Values and Attitudes

Purpose: To move the conflict positions of the parties to the core of their conflict, and identify needs and underlying interests.

Future Focus Questions
Hypothetical, Conditional, Consequential, BATNA / MLATNA / WATNA

Purpose: To move parties off the conflict treadmill and facilitate cognitive thinking, leading to options and solutions.

Figure: 15.1.
CREDIT: O'SULLIVAN SOLUTIONS

S4: Other People Questions

OTHER PEOPLE QUESTIONS support parties to reflect by exploring an imagined perspective of the other party, a third party, a cultural norm, or hypothetical parties outside the current paradigm of their conflict.

How Do Other People Questions Work?

Other People questions provide a safe way to ask difficult questions that broaden the perspectives of parties and makes it easier for them to respond to questions which might otherwise invoke a feeling of threat.

When a party does not easily engage with a direct question, it may be easier for them to talk from a third-party perspective. When this question is accompanied by open and respectful body language, it will facilitate a party to think cognitively, rather than being defensive and adopting an avoid-threat reflex.

> Example:
>
> Instead of asking:
>
> > What are the things that you find difficult to manage in your work?
>
> It may be less threatening to ask:
>
> > What are the things your teammates find difficult to manage at work?
> >
> > How do other team members manage these difficulties?
> >
> > What parts do you find the most difficult and how would that compare with the parts that others might find difficult?
> >
> > How do other team members manage these difficulties?

When to Ask Other People Questions

Other people questions are used:

- ✓ When a question could inadvertently result in a party experiencing an avoid-threat reflex
- ✓ When little understanding has been reached between parties
- ✓ When a party may be anxious and may view a question as exposing their vulnerability to the other party
- ✓ When a safe space needs to be created for parties to slowly consider the possibilities of other options or solutions, without making the commitment that they are not ready to make yet
- ✓ When it may be necessary to expand a party's thinking to provide alternatives for solution

Methodology

The body language and tone of voice used by the mediator in asking this type of question is crucial. They need to be very gentle, while adding a light sprinkling of curiosity, so that their questions are not seen as judgmental or manipulative.

Before being asked Other People questions, parties need to have ample time to air their emotions and issues. If a party seems to be unable to experience or express any empathy for the other party, or if they have not sufficiently expressed their emotions, the responses they may give may be damaging to the other party. For instance:

> Mediator's question:
>
> How do you think the conflict may have impacted the other party?

> Party's response:
>
> How should I know?! Anyway, this conflict is all their fault and they should have considered the consequences before they did what they did last week!

Building Other People Questions

Other People questions can be built and asked using one of several methods, where a mediator invites a respondent to take on the perspective of another person when answering the question:

Method 1: Hypothetical questions asked of Party A about Party B

Method 2: The perspective of conflict observers

Method 3: The perspective of a cultural norm

Method 4: A hypothetical perspective from outside the current paradigm

Hazard Warning

The first separate private meetings need to be used to explore Other People questions to ascertain whether asking them when parties are in the room together is going to be safe.

Case study as the context for illustrating examples of S4: Other People questions

A SEPARATED COUPLE AND PARENTAL ACCESS

Beth will not allow her ex-husband, Bob, to have access to their child (Joey, aged nine) unless her own mother is in attendance as well. She says that Bob is irresponsible and is unable to look after Joey properly. Bob says that he is well able to look after Joey and that Beth is just angry and jealous because he kept the child longer than was agreed the last time he had access, and because he spends more time having fun with Joey than he spends feeding and cleaning him.

Questions That May Be Asked Prior to Using the Four Different Other People Questions Methods

Introductory questions:

- Beth, you mentioned that you think Bob is irresponsible. In what way do you think he does not behave responsibly when taking care of Joey?
- Can you give any examples of what concerns you the most?
- Are there specific times or contexts in which you find that Bob is more responsible?
- What are the parts of the parenting role where you feel that Bob does manage very well?
- What are the parts of the parenting role where you feel that Bob does not manage very well?

Impact and emotions questions:

- What is it like for you to be in this situation when you are doubting Joey's dad's capacity?
- What might be your deep-down worries about all this?

Underlying Interests questions:

If the answers to these questions demonstrate to the mediator that there is some room for flexibility in this situation, and if the mediator learns that Beth is holding her position from an underlying interest fear that Joey may start to prefer his dad more than his mom, or any other possible underlying interest, rather than because she sees Bob as being irresponsible and a danger to Joey, then the first task is to allow Beth to express her emotions and concerns about this and to facilitate her to get down to her underlying interests. When this is achieved, the climate may be conducive to asking Beth some Other People questions about their child being with his father. Let's go through each of the four methods of asking Other People questions with this issue.

Method 1: Hypothetical Questions Asked of Party A about Party B

Asking Other People questions directly of one party about the other party is used if moderate empathy toward the other party has been demonstrated from the party being asked the question.

These Other People questions support one party to think the issue through from the perspective of the other party. The party who is asked the question will need to clarify their thinking before responding, and this reflection may lead to new insight. If this happens, and if this takes place at a joint meeting, the party who is hearing the responses will know that the other party is beginning to understand their perspective.

It is important that these questions are first checked out at a separate private meeting, in case they result in a response such as:

Well, if I was in Beth's shoes, I wouldn't have reacted like she did!

These questions can be asked in two ways:

a) Hypothetical questions that are directly asked of one party, who takes on the imagined perspective of the other party

b) Hypothetical questions that are directly asked of one party about what it would be like if they were actually that other party

a) Hypothetical questions that are directly asked of one party, who takes on the imagined perspective of the other party

Examples:

After Bob has talked about his situation and the impact it is having on him, Other People questions can be asked:

Bob, if you were in Beth's shoes, with ***her*** *thoughts, feelings, experiences and perspectives* rather than your own:

- What do you think is happening for Beth when she says she does not wish you to take care of Joey unless her mother is in attendance?
- When did you realize that this was an issue for Beth? How did Beth display it?
- What do you think may have caused Beth's behavior/reaction?

Asking S4: Journey of Inference questions linked to Other People questions:

Bob, you mentioned that Beth tells you that you spend too much time playing with Joey and that she says you don't give him proper healthy dinners:

- How do you think Beth interprets the fact that you spend a lot of time playing with Joey?
- What might she assume will happen?
- What conclusion might she have come to?
- What might have been Beth's experience of life that would lead her to this conclusion?
- How do you think this may be impacting on Beth?
- How could that influence Beth's decisions and actions?

Switch back to asking direct questions of Bob:

- What was it like being asked these questions, Bob?
- What might you wish Beth to know?
- What are all your possible options?

<hr>

Hazard Warning

To reduce the likelihood of an inflammatory reaction when asking Other People questions, it is important to ask the party to **think** like the other party **with that other party's thoughts, feelings and perspectives**, rather than thinking about what they themselves would have done if they had been in those circumstances. It is very common that parties slip back into blame when asked Other People questions, so it is very important for a mediator to stay focused with these questions to avoid deviation from the task.

b) Hypothetical questions that are directly asked of one party about what it would be like if they were actually that other party

These questions challenge the parties to get into the space of the other and experience the other's situation.

These questions can also be used to interchange parties' specific feelings.

Example:

Asking Beth what it would be like for **her** if Bob did not trust her to take care of their children is another effective way of helping the parties to understand each other. Again, these questions may need to be well managed so they are not seen by Beth as being either threatening or manipulating, and they need to be first tested at a separate meeting.

Examples:

Beth, I would like you to imagine something — if Bob had the opinion that **you** were not behaving responsibly with Joey, and that your time with Joey needed to be supervised.

- What would that be like for you?
- What would be the worst thing about it for you?
- What would this be like for Joey?
- What might you want to happen?

Switch back to asking direct questions of Beth:

- What was it like being asked these questions, Beth?
- What might you wish Bob to know?
- What are all your possible options?

Method 2: The Perspective of Conflict Observers

This type of Other People question is asked of one party about the possible perspectives of external conflict observers in the environment or context in which the conflict is taking place. Asking questions about third parties who observed an incident, or who are also living or working within the conflict situation, can be an important and safe tool to expand the thinking of the parties in conflict. The conflict observers in this case study could be relatives or friends of Bob and Beth, neighbors or even their son, Joey.

Examples:

From what Joey has observed and experienced about your relationship with each other:

- How might Joey describe what is happening?
- What meaning do you think Joey might take from what is happening between the two of you?
- What might Joey be afraid could happen?
- What conclusions or judgment might Joey have come to?
- What might Joey be worrying about?
- How could these worries impact on him in the short term? In the long term?
- What could Joey want each of you to do to address his worries?

Switch back to asking direct questions of both Bob and Beth:

- What could all this mean for you?
- What might you wish Joey to know?
- What might Joey need to hear from you?

Method 3: The Perspective of a Cultural Norm

The sample questions here are being asked about other similar couples in the community of Beth and Bob. But they can also be asked from the perspective of the cultural norm of either of the parties, particularly if parties do not share the same race or religious or ethnic background.

Examples:

- Beth and Bob, how do you think other couples in your community manage their coparenting in conflictual situations of separation or divorce?
- How do you see others in your community react in situations like this? What might inform or influence their reactions?
- What might other people in your community try to achieve in a situation like this?
- How might they manage it? What would they do? How would they do it?
- How is this either the same or different to what you could do?
- How could you use this information?

Switch back to asking direct questions of Bob and Beth:

- What does all this mean for you, Bob and Beth?
- What might you wish each other to know?
- What, if any, actions would you like to take?
- What are all your possible options?

Method 4: Hypothetical Perspective from Outside the Current Paradigm

Asking Other People questions from outside the parties' current paradigm, in a hypothetical way, can help if there is little empathy or understanding between one party and another.

These questions can be asked in either of two ways:

a) From the perspective of a hypothetical third party

b) As if the respondent party is the hypothetical observer of their own conflict

a) Questions asked from the perspective of a hypothetical third party

The following technique can be used if there is still some intransigence or resistance from Beth, but during a private meeting.

Examples:

- Beth, how do you think a hypothetical person, who is outside all of this and does not know either of you, might view your decision that Bob cannot be with your child unless your mother is also in attendance?
- If this hypothetical person was to say that **you** were not a responsible parent, what would you need this hypothetical person to say before you would believe what they said?
- What else do you think could be of concern to them that perhaps they might not be willing to say?
- What might this hypothetical person need to hear that would allay their concerns?

When these questions are well managed, and when the party's response shows some understanding, it can have a powerful effect on the party who is listening if they are asked at the joint meeting. The party who is listening begins to realize that perhaps the other party understands their experiences and perspectives a little more than they had envisioned. This may result in them feeling less threatened and therefore less anxious to hold on to their position.

b) Questions asked as if a party is the hypothetical observer of their own conflict

Another method to use is to ask a party to become the "observer" of their own conflict. These questions support a party, such as Beth, to step outside their situation and look at the conflict with a potentially new perspective.

Examples using a Journey of Inference questions flow:

- Beth, if you had been observing from a balcony the conversations that you have had with Bob about needing your mother to be in attendance when he was with Joey, what might you have observed about Bob? What might you have observed about yourself?
- How would you interpret what you saw?
- What assumptions might you have made about what might happen?
- What conclusions might you have come to?
- What advice would you give to this couple?
- What might you suggest to Bob?
- What might you suggest to Beth?
- What do you see, from the balcony, that these two people could offer to each other?

Switch back to asking direct questions of Beth:

- What does all this mean for you, Beth?
- What might you wish Bob to know?
- What, if any, actions would you like to take?
- What are all your possible options?

Key Learning

OTHER PEOPLE QUESTIONS

Other People questions support parties to reflect by facilitating them to make connections with the perspective of either the other party, or with an external perspective or a cultural norm, or with a hypothetical perspective that is outside the current paradigm of their conflict.

Other People questions can be built and asked using several methods where a mediator invites a respondent to take on another person's perspective while answering the questions.

Method 1: Hypothetical questions asked of party A about party B

a) Hypothetical questions that are directly asked of one party, who takes on the imagined perspective of the other party.

b) Hypothetical questions that are directly asked of one party about what it would be like if they were actually that other party.

Method 2: The perspective of conflict observers
This type of Other People question is asked of one party about the possible perspectives of external conflict observers in the environment or context in which the conflict is taking place.

Method 3: The perspective of a cultural norm
These questions are asked from the perspective of the cultural norm of either of the parties, or of the cultural norm of the environment / context in which the conflict takes place.

Method 4: A hypothetical perspective from outside the current paradigm

a) Questions asked from the perspective of a hypothetical third party.

b) Questions asked as if a party is the hypothetical observer of their own conflict.

Hazard Warning

It is important to reiterate here that these questions may need to be tested during the initial separate private meeting or in a private meeting during a joint session.

Hazard Warning

Do not pressure a party to answer a question — proceed carefully and gently, at their pace, and with their permission.

S4: Underlying Interests Questions

16

S4: The Shift Thinking Dimension of Questions — Underlying Interests Questions

(For background information, refer to the theoretical input in Chapter 3: Working with the Brain in Mediation.)

S4: The Shift Thinking Dimension of Questions

To uncover new information and insight, either by exploring and focusing thinking or by connecting and expanding thinking, leading to a paradigm shift

Journey of Inference Questions
Interpretations, Assumptions, Conclusions, Beliefs, Actions

Purpose: To identify the link between interpretations and actions. To explore parties' current narratives and to shift perspectives toward a new narrative.

Neuro-linguistic Programming (NLP) Based Questions
Deletions, Distortions, Generalizations

Purpose: To bring clarity; explore subjective realities, explore bias and misinterpretations, and create congruency in communication.

Distinction and Difference Questions
People, Parts, Contexts, Opposites, Spatial, Comparisons, Time Span, Measurement or Ranking

Purpose: To bring clarity, relevance, measurement, boundary and a different perspective to the conflict.

Reflective Connecting Questions
Connecting with patterns and cycles of conflict, both intrapersonal and interpersonal, and in the broader context

Purpose: To raise awareness of negative patterns and cycles of conflict, to deconstruct past unhelpful patterns and to reconstruct new healthy patterns.

Cognitive Elements-based Questions
Knowledge; Opinion and Thinking; Beliefs, Values and Attitudes; Behaviour; Sense of Self/Identity; Environment

Purpose: To explore inner conflicts and inconsistencies between perception and reality, and between the six cognitive elements. To seek a paradigm shift that will restore cognitive consonance.

Other People Questions
Explore an imagined perspective of the other party, a third party, a cultural norm or hypothetical parties

Purpose: To open perspectives and create insight safely.

Underlying Interests Questions
Conflict Triggers, Impact, Beliefs, Values and Attitudes

Purpose: To move the conflict positions of the parties to the core of their conflict, and identify needs and underlying interests.

Future Focus Questions
Hypothetical, Conditional, Consequential, BATNA / MLATNA / WATNA

Purpose: To move parties off the conflict treadmill and facilitate cognitive thinking, leading to options and solutions.

Figure: 16.1.

S4: Underlying Interests Questions

UNDERLYING INTERESTS QUESTIONS delve beneath the conflict positions and demands presented by parties in mediation. They are designed to reach the core of their conflict and discover the things that are important to them. Getting to the underlying interests introduces new and valuable information to a mediation process and creates new insight and understanding between parties in conflict. This in turn should lead to a paradigm shift in their thinking and approach toward the conflict and toward each other.

When the needs and underlying interests of parties have been identified, they will feel more understood, be able to think cognitively and therefore be ready to move to identifying sustainable solutions that meet their underlying interests. Once the underlying interests have been reached, there is no need to remain focused on the parties' past experiences for any longer than is necessary. However, it is important to discuss the past for long enough to facilitate parties to vent their feelings, explore their underlying interests and then use these past experiences as a platform from which to identify and explore options for the future.

Theoretical Background

The Definitions of Issue, Position and Underlying Interest

Prior to exploring how to unearth the underlying interests of a party, it is necessary to look at what is meant by the mediation terms *issue, position* and *underlying interest.*

Issue

An issue is the subject matter of the conflict that requires resolution.

Position

A position is the stance a party takes to the conflict in which they are involved. This is the place from where they rationalize their situation and then act and react. When a party is feeling vulnerable, the *position* they take may become fixed and will be their way of protecting that vulnerability. There is a need to draw a distinction between a *position* and a *fixed position.* Adopting a position is not in itself problematic, but when a party sticks firmly to their position, then the situation becomes more difficult to solve.

The position taken by a party may include:

- Defending themselves by blaming the other person
- Making demands, such as saying, "Either she goes or I go!"
- Insisting on an apology
- Continuing to believe that the other party wants to damage them, even when evidence contradicts this belief

POSITIONS

A *position* is the stance
that a party takes in a conflict.

External / Conscious

Examples of positional language:

'I want...'

'She has to change her attitude
or else...!'

'I refuse to have anything
more to do with him...'

UNDERLYING INTERESTS

An *underlying interest* is a conscious or
unconscious need within a person that
they protect by taking the position or
stance that they adopt.

The motivation for protecting this need
may be triggered by a threat to their
values or beliefs, or to their SCARF® Drivers
of status, certainty, autonomy,
relatedness, fairness.

Internal / Unconscious*

*The more emotionally intelligent a person is, the less
the activity under the waterline will be unconscious

© www.osullivansolutions.ie

Figure: 16.2.

Underlying Interest

An underlying interest is a conscious or unconscious need or vulnerability within a person that they protect by taking a position or stance to protect themselves. It is this deep-down need or fear that informs and drives the stance or position that a party adopts in conflict. The motivation to protect these underlying interests may be caused by a threat to the values or beliefs that are very important to them, or to their SCARF® Drivers of status, certainty, autonomy, relatedness or fairness.

The positions adopted and stated by the parties are the gateways to their underlying interests. It is important to note and explore these identified positions, with their accompanying displayed emotions, to get to the underlying interests of a party. It is by addressing these unseen layers that conflict can be transformed effectively and sustainably.

How Do Underlying Interests Questions Work?

When people engage in mediation, they begin with their narrative fully embedded and demonstrate this narrative with the conflict position that they take. The positions adopted and stated by the parties, and the emotions they display, are the key to uncovering their underlying interests. Exploring what is *beneath* a party's position is what will lead to increased understanding for both parties and to an appropriate, sustainable and effective resolution.

Asking Underlying Interests questions sensitively, and with integrity, helps parties to identify and verbalize their emotions. Chapter 3 described the concept of affect labeling: if people verbalize their emotions, this produces diminished responses in their amygdala and other limbic regions. It is crucial to facilitate parties to verbalize their emotions so that they can then start to think cognitively before exploring any possible options or agreements.

Case study: Getting past positions to underlying interests

To illustrate getting beneath parties' positions to reach their needs and underlying interests

ISSUE

A local authority housing officer had difficulty with what he perceived as unrealistic demands from residents in a housing estate. On the other hand, the residents felt that their request was perfectly reasonable and should be met.

POSITION OF HOUSING OFFICER

The housing officer had spent two years telling the residents that it was not possible to give them a playground, for three reasons:

1. There was already a playground in that small town.

2. He could not set a precedent, because if he did, every other small local authority estate would demand a playground.

3. There was no money in the budget of the local authority for this work.

POSITION OF RESIDENTS

The residents wanted a playground in their small estate. They maintained that they had been asking the local authority for a playground for two years and they were no longer accepting any reasons for the refusal of their request.

A mediator was invited to work with the parties and asked the residents the following questions:

- What would your request (position) in asking for a playground give you?

- What are your concerns and worries? (underlying interests)

- What needs of yours are not being met? (underlying interests)

- If you had a playground, what would it give you? (underlying interests)

UNDERLYING INTERESTS OF RESIDENTS

After exploring these questions with the residents, it became clear that the residents had two main reasons for requesting a playground:

1. That the area of grass in their housing estate where they wanted a playground to be located becomes very muddy when it rains, resulting in the children becoming wet and dirty.

2. That the perimeter of this area of grass was surrounded by a road and the parents worried that a child would be knocked down by a car if they ran onto the road running after a ball.

After some more exploration, it transpired that the residents wanted the grassy area covered with the type of surface material that is used in a playground, so their children would not get wet and muddy, and they wanted a low wall built around the perimeter of this area of grass, so that the children could not run directly onto the road when running after a ball. They did not actually want swings and slides but needed what the structure and surface of a playground would give them.

The response from the local authority housing officer was:

But it is no problem to do that for you! I thought you wanted a playground?!

When to Ask Underlying Interests Questions

These questions are used:

✓ When parties hold steadfastly to their conflict positions and demands

✓ When a mediator needs to move the parties beyond their conflict positions to the root cause of their negative emotions

✓ When a mediator is unsure of the reason and the extent that a conflict situation has impacted on a party

✓ When parties do not understand why the conflict is causing them such inner stress

✓ When the emotional distress of a party is blocking progress in the mediation

✓ To facilitate parties to gain new insight and understanding

✓ To get to the core of the conflict to identify the underlying interests of the parties so that appropriate and sustainable solutions that match these underlying interests can be found

Methodology

While Chapter 4 contains generic guidelines for asking questions, there are additional specific guidelines for Underlying Interests questions.

Guidelines for Asking Underlying Interests Questions

At the initial separate meeting, assess the appropriateness of asking Underlying Interests questions, before asking a party these questions during a joint meeting.

- Do not ask one party about their underlying interests until *both* parties have told their stories and have vented their anger or negative emotions; otherwise the party who has not yet been heard will not be willing or able to listen cognitively.

- If a party seems incapable of expressing empathy for the other party, then exercise caution about exposing the vulnerability of either party.

- Do not push parties past their comfort zone as not all parties may wish to delve into deeper areas.

- Work with parties in a way that is appropriate to the field of mediation by facilitating them to find a future without the problems of the past. Do not begin to take on the role of a counselor or psychotherapist.

- If parties do not need to have a relationship with each other after mediation, this might reduce the need to explore underlying interests fully; however, it may still need to be done if reaching an agreement is dependent on the parties having a deeper understanding of what went wrong in the past.

Methodology for Asking and Developing
S4: Underlying Interests Questions

1. Use appropriate body language
2. Signpost and set the tone for asking Underlying Interests questions
3. Gently reflect back what you are hearing at the start of the process
4. Facilitate the expression of emotions, unobtrusively
5. Identify and use the last words voiced by a party
6. Recognize the difference between positional statements and underlying interests statements
7. Recognize underlying interest feelings within positional statements
8. Support a party who is hesitant to reveal their underlying interests
9. Be aware of the indicators that demonstrate that underlying interests have been reached
10. Work with knowledge of the avoid-threat reflex
11. Ask S4: Future Focus questions after the underlying interests of *both* parties have been explored

1. Use Appropriate Body Language

Use body language that will indicate nonverbally to a party that the tone of the mediation is going to change:

- Put any notes or notepad away.
- Ensure that you are seated and lean in toward the party, but do not move into their intimate space.
- Lower the level of your voice and speak gently, slowly and quietly.

2. Signpost and Set the Tone for Asking Underlying Interests Questions

Prior to exploring underlying interests, the mediator signposts what they are going to do next:

> I am going to ask each of you how this conflict has impacted on you. I would like to ask Jean some questions, and I would like you, Dan, to really listen, and then I will do the same with you, Dan, and I will ask Jean to listen.

3. Gently Reflect Back What You Are Hearing at the Start of the Process

At the start of the process of exploring underlying interests, a mediator needs to reflect back what was said by the party prior to asking another question. However, as the discussion becomes more exploratory and deeper, the need for reflecting back what you have heard is greatly reduced and a mediator need only reflect back an important feeling word such as "devastated," or just nod their head. To do otherwise would interrupt the party's flow of thoughts. The mediator, in that quiet and deeper space, needs to be completely in the moment with that party so they can go on their journey of thoughts, feelings and explorations.

4. Facilitate the Expression of Emotions, Unobtrusively

If a party is not comfortable expressing their emotions, then asking them directly about how they are feeling may be seen as intrusive by them, and they may feel threatened and block the conversation. In this case, there may be a need to translate questions about feelings in a way that is seen by parties as being less touchy-feely or intrusive,

Examples:

- How were you affected by that?
- What was it like for you when that happened?
- What reaction did that generate in you?
- What was the worst thing about all of that for you?
- What has been the impact on you?
- What is the one word that would adequately describe the impact on you when that happened?

Note:
Avoid asking a party questions such as "How did that *make* you feel?" as the other party may perceive this as the mediator blaming them. A mediator needs to work on the basis that each party is responsible for their own feelings and reactions to the behavior of the other.

5. Identify and Use the Last Words Voiced by a Party

When parties are describing their experiences, the last words they use before they stop talking can often be their own unconscious summary of their truth, what has happened, what is important to them and how they are feeling about it. This can be a gateway to their underlying interests and can be used to formulate the next underlying interests question:

Example:

Party:

> ...and that was why I made the complaint, I couldn't take it anymore.

Mediator:

- You mention that you could not take it anymore, what was it that you could not take any more?
- What was it like for you to be in a place where you say you could not take it anymore?

6. Recognize the Difference Between Positional Statements and Underlying Interest Statements

A positional statement is blaming and demanding and is usually delivered with negative emotions and body language. On the other hand, an underlying interest statement illustrates how a person is feeling about what has happened, and what the impact has been on them. It is usually delivered in a quieter manner.

Example:

> There is a difference between when a party says "I can't sleep" using an aggressive and positional tone, and when they use the same words — "I can't sleep" — quietly and calmly, as an expression of the difficulties they are experiencing in the conflict.

Examples of Differences Between Positional Statements and Underlying Interests Statements

Statement	Approach	Words
Positional statement	Blames and demands Uses aggressive body language Uses sharp and loud tone of voice	I JUST CAN'T SLEEP ANYMORE! SHE SHOULD GET ON WITH HER OWN WORK AND STOP BOTHERING ME!!!!
Underlying interest statement	Describes the impact Uses gentle but firm body language Uses quieter and softer tone of voice	I just can't sleep anymore and feel frightened when she comes toward me with a question, because I might not know the answer — this is causing me a lot of stress and sleepless nights.

The reason it is important to identify the difference between a positional statement and an underlying interest statement is that sometimes when a mediator starts to explore underlying interests, a party can easily slip back up into a positional stance and the opportunity to continue to bring them down to underlying interests may seem to be lost.

To manage this, and only after the parties have had time to vent their feelings, a mediator needs to ignore the positional language statements and gently bring the party back to their underlying interests statements:

> Mediator: You mentioned that you are not sleeping, what is that like for you?
>
> Party: It's devastating (said in a quiet voice) AND IT'S ALL HER FAULT (said angrily)
>
> Mediator: In what way is it devastating?
>
> Party: I am exhausted every day and can't manage the work. SHE HAS TO STOP!
>
> Mediator: What is it like for you to feel exhausted and not be able to manage your work?

...and continue until underlying interests are reached and the party has become noticeably calmer.

7. Recognize Underlying Interest Feelings Within Positional Statements

Underlying interest feeling statements may be contained within positional statements or interspersed within the narrative of a party. It is important to listen carefully for feeling statements that might indicate underlying interests so that they can be captured and used in questions to get beneath the positional level of a party.

> Example of a party expressing an underlying sentiment within their positional statement:
>
> Party:
>
> > She should not have done that! This is not normal behavior and I have never come across anything like it before. *I felt completely powerless!* This is outlandish behavior and would not be tolerated anywhere else.
>
> Mediator:
>
> > You mentioned that you felt completely powerless ... powerless in what way? What has this been like for you? How has it impacted on you? What was the worst thing for you about feeling powerless? What were you worried about for the future?

8. Support a Party Who Is Hesitant to Reveal Their Underlying Interests

In some cases, a party may not feel comfortable expressing their underlying interests in front of the party with whom they are in conflict. It is very important to not pressure them on this issue. But in some instances, the parties may have had a previous relationship, and reaching underlying interests may increase understanding between them.

Note:
Initially, these questions may need to be asked at a separate private meeting during the joint meeting.

Note:
Refer to osullivansolutions.ie for a film that demonstrates how to create a safe space for a party to open up during a joint session.

Examples:

- Dan, I note that you are not comfortable about opening up opposite the other party; what is it that concerns you? What are you worried about?

- What might you lose by not saying it? What might you gain by saying it?

- How important is it to you that understanding be created between you? What mark out of 10 would you rate this importance?

- What are all the ways in which your concerns about opening up could be alleviated?

- What would you need to know or understand from the other party before you would feel comfortable? If you had that assurance from them, how would it help? What might you need to ask from the other party so you would feel comfortable about opening up?

9. Be Aware of the Indicators That Demonstrate That Underlying Interests Have Been Reached

You will know that the underlying interests of parties have been reached when a party is no longer acting from their original positional state, has become less positional and cathartically quieter in their tone, starts to use fewer words or responds in a monosyllabic manner.

Example:

After several questions to bring to the surface underlying interests, a party may indicate a final emotion by just saying, "It… was… devastating."

Or they may even respond by merely nodding their head and staying silent as a means of acknowledging that the mediation questions have reached the core of their problem and they have nothing more to say. If you think that the underlying interests have been reached, and that there is no new insight to be gained, then just remain silent to give both parties time to reflect on what has been said. One of them will take the initiative to speak when they are ready. Often it is the party who has been listening that starts to contribute. They may start by saying how shocked they are to hear what has just been said, that they had no idea of the impact on the other party, etc. It is very important that the mediator captures this immediately and reflects it back to the party whose underlying interests have been reached so that it has the required impact. This is done effectively by the mediator looking at that party while reflecting back what the other party has said.

10. Work with Knowledge of the Avoid-threat Reflex

Once underlying interests have been reached, refrain from focusing on the past for any longer than is necessary as this may activate the avoid-threat reflex and result in an amygdala hijack. All it takes is for one party to repeat something from the old narrative, such as "He really should not have done that!" to spark the other party into responding defensively and counterattacking, and if this is allowed to grow and fester, it will unravel all the good work that has been achieved. It may just take a few seconds to unravel but could take two hours for a mediator to bring the parties back on track again!

You might say that surely if underlying interests have been uncovered effectively then this should not happen, and you would be right to do so as it could mean this that this needs to be checked out. However, when parties have lived within a narrative for many months or years of conflict, it takes time before they start to trust each other and let the old narrative go. In other words, they are still protecting themselves to a certain extent as they have no concrete evidence yet that things have changed, so a mediator needs to ensure that once underlying interests have been reached that past emotions are not inadvertently or unnecessarily raised, risking a deviation from the journey of building a new and alternative narrative.

11. Ask S4: Future Focus Questions After the Underlying Interests of Both Parties Have Been Explored

Once parties have vented their emotions, underlying interests have been identified and understanding has been reached, and there is no new information or insight to be gained, a mediator needs to switch to asking S4: Future Focus questions to find the way forward and create a new narrative. It is very important that this is managed tightly, as a party can easily slip back into their former negative narrative, which will result in the conversations going around in circles without a conclusion.

> Future Focus question example:
>> You mentioned that this was a very difficult time for you, and you said you were very worried that you would lose your job and not be able to keep up the mortgage repayments and provide for your family … what needs to be put in place now so that you have a firm agreement that will ensure that you no longer have these worries?

S4: Future Focus questions are covered in Chapter 17, the next chapter.

How to Build Conscious Underlying Interests and Unconscious Underlying Interests Questions

The underlying interests of a party may be conscious and easy to identify, or may be unconscious and require additional methods to discover them.

Difference Between Conscious and Unconscious Underlying Interests

It is the role of the mediator to facilitate parties to be clear about what they wish to say in mediation. When a party is at a strong positional level, this is when their negative emotions are displayed, and it is beneath these negative emotions that their unsaid underlying interests can be discovered.

There are many layers of underlying interests beneath a party's position. Asking parties what attaining their positional demand will give them may be sufficient to reach conscious underlying interests. However, in some situations, a party may not know their underlying interests, as these remain at their unconscious level, so unearthing them may not be quite so easy. The presence of unconscious underlying interests will be demonstrated by a party's confusion about the unexpected impact the conflict has had on them.

Parties may say things like:

- I cannot believe the impact this is having on me! I don't know what is going on!

or

- I can't see any way out of this. It's all completely hopeless.

Unconscious or less obvious underlying interests need additional methods. These methods ask parties about the event that triggered their response when they first became aware that there was a conflict, what negative emotions arose for them as a result of the trigger, what SCARF® Drivers were impacted or how their values or beliefs seemed to be threatened.

Note:
The above questioning methods do not always need to be used in the order in which they are listed here, but their use needs to be relevant to the particular discussion that is taking place.

Question tasks for uncovering Underlying Interests: Both conscious and unconscious

Conscious underlying interests Generic questions	Unconscious underlying interests Additional questions
Conflict positions?	Conflict trigger and the emotional response to it?
Impact?	Impact on SCARF® Drivers?
Emotions?	Values and beliefs?
Concerns/worries?	
Conscious needs?	

(i) Conscious Underlying Interests with Questions

The time that passes from when the amygdala detects a threat to the time a party adopts a position is only a split second. A party's positional demands are usually voiced as a protection mechanism and often disappear when their underlying interests have been voiced and heard and when understanding has been reached between parties.

The type of position that a party takes is influenced by their past experiences of conflict, the way they view conflict and the values and beliefs they have formed. This is the place from where they rationalize their situation and react. The positions they take are their negative expressions of what they really need: what they determine will protect them.

Conscious underlying interests Generic questions
Conflict positions?
Impact?
Emotions?
Concerns/worries?
Conscious needs?

The above questioning methods do not always need to be used in the order in which they are listed here, but their use needs to be relevant to the particular discussion that is taking place.

Generic Questions

A) Questions to Ask About What a Party's Positional Demand Could Achieve for Them

You can explore beneath a party's positional statement by asking about what their positional demand could give them if it was met:

Party: I want him sacked immediately! (Positional statement)

The mediator then looks for underlying interests by asking what a party's positional demand could give them, if it was met:

Mediator: If your boss was sacked, what would this give you? What specific needs of yours would be addressed?

Party: Then the bullying would stop. (Underlying interest)

Mediator: If the behavior of your boss was different, what would that give you? Specifically, what do you need from your boss?

B) QUESTIONS TO ASK ABOUT THE IMPACT THAT THE CONFLICT HAS HAD ON PARTIES

When parties are asked about the impact a conflict has had on them, this facilitates them to start talking about the emotional aspect of the conflict, which can be the gateway to identifying the core of their conflict.

Examples:

- Will you tell me a little about the impact this has had on you?
- How would you describe this impact?
- What exactly was impacted?
- In what way was it impacted?
- What has been the worst thing about this impact on you?
- What are you worried might happen if this impact continues into the future?

C) QUESTIONS TO ASK ABOUT EMOTIONS

Parties need to be asked what emotions surfaced for them during the conflict.

Examples:

- What was all this like for you?
- How were you affected by it?
- What was the main feeling response that you had?
- What was the worst thing about this for you?
- What is the one word that could describe your feelings?

D) QUESTIONS TO ASK ABOUT CONCERNS AND WORRIES

Parties need to explore their concerns or worries.

Examples:

- What are the concerns or worries you have had around this, both now and for the future?
- What are your priority concerns?
- What is the depth of your concerns? 0 = not deep and 10 = very deep
- What was it about this concern that made it a particular worry for you?
- What were you worried might happen at that time?
- What specifically are you worried about right now?
- What are you worried might happen in the future?

E) QUESTIONS TO ASK ABOUT THE NEEDS OF THE PARTIES

Parties can be asked about any of their needs that were not met.

Examples:

- What needs of yours were not met at the start of the conflict? What needs are not being met now? What needs are you worried may not be met in the future?

- Can you identify the level of importance of each need and the reason you give it this level of importance? What might happen if your most important needs are not addressed?

- In what other ways could your needs be met? (Note: other than by their positional demands)

- What would be the outcome for both of you if these needs were met?

Case study: Getting to conscious underlying interests

Speaker	Stages of the process	Dialogue between the mediator and party
Party	Party at blaming position	She has ruined my sleep for the last two months! She should adhere to the guidelines and then there wouldn't be a problem. I want her moved to a different department!
Mediator	Checking what the achievement of the positional demand would give	If Jean was moved to a different department, what would this give you?
Party	Starting to explore underling interests	Well, I would no longer need to worry about her not adhering to the guidelines!
Mediator	Identifying impact and emotions	How does it impact on you when the guidelines are not adhered to? What is this like for you? How do you feel about this?
Mediator	Identifying concerns, worries, needs	When you are uncertain about what is going to happen, what is it that concerns you the most? What needs of yours are not being met?
Party	Identifying emotions and underlying interests	We might lose our biggest client.
Mediator	Identifying worries and concerns to explore emotions further	And when you say you are afraid that you may lose your biggest client, what is this like for you?
Party	Identifying emotions	It's awful, I don't sleep well and am constantly tired and not able to concentrate on anything properly.
Mediator	Identifying worries about the deeper impact	And what is it about this that concerns you the most?
Party	Exploring emotions and underlying interests	I am afraid we will lose more clients and go out of business.
Mediator	Identifying emotional impact	What would this be like for you?
Party	Deeper underlying interests	Terrible.
Mediator	Gently and quietly repeating the word and leaving it hang in case the party needs to say more	Terrible?
Party	Deeper underlying interests	Yes, and I would be unable to keep up the mortgage payments as my wife has been made redundant.
Mediator	Identifying the depth of the emotions	You're worried? What is this like for you? What is the worst thing about it?
Party	Identifying the emotions and getting to deeper underlying interests	It would be devastating…. I mean, a man is supposed to to be the provider for the family.
Mediator	Hearing the depth of the emotions	Devastating.
Party	Underling interests are reached when party responds by saying "Yes" or "That's it," or if they just nod their head and stay silent	Yeah…. (Said with a huge sigh and followed by reflective silence.)

(ii) Unconscious Underlying Interests with Questions

To identify and reach unconscious underlying interests, there are some additional specific methods that can be used.

Note:

At times it may not be necessary to go to deeper underlying interests. A mediator needs to make a judgment on what depth is appropriate in any given context.

Unconscious underlying interests Additional questions
Conflict trigger and the emotional response to it?
Impact on SCARF® Drivers?
Values and beliefs?

Additional Methods for Identifying Unconscious Underlying Interests

METHOD 1: EXPLORE CONFLICT TRIGGERS [44]

Identify the stimulus or triggering event that resulted in a party's disproportionate negative emotional response. When we have a sudden and disproportionate emotional reaction to a stimulus, this brings to the fore the fact that another's values, beliefs, needs, interests, assumptions or perceptions are incompatible with ours. Then support the party to identify the connection between this stimulus and their reactions, and to explore the emotions that surfaced for them as a result of the stimulus.

METHOD 2: EXPLORE SCARF® DRIVERS THAT MAY HAVE BEEN IMPACTED

Identify whether there has been any impact on any of the SCARF® Drivers of status, certainty, autonomy, relatedness and fairness (David Rock). These drivers can then be used as questioning subjects for exploring unconscious needs.

METHOD 3: EXPLORE VALUES AND BELIEFS

Explore the values and beliefs of the parties to ascertain what is important to them and identify what has actually been impacted or threatened, or what they *perceive* to have been threatened.

These three methods do not always need to be used in the order in which they are listed here. Choose a method depending on the areas of discussion that are taking place between the parties.

Examples:

- If a party has started to describe the impact on one of their values, then asking questions about this impact on their beliefs and values, followed by questions regarding any loss from this, would be appropriate at that time.

or

- If a party is talking about how the conflict started, then asking conflict trigger questions would be more appropriate.

The rest of this chapter has examples of questions that can be asked for each of the three methods to identify the unconscious underlying interests.

Method 1: Exploring Conflict Triggers to Reach Unconscious Underlying Interests

A conflict trigger is an event that results in a sudden and disproportionate emotional response in a person. This emotional response indicates that something of fundamental value to the person is perceived to be, or is, under threat. Identifying the trigger for this threat response, with its accompanying disproportionate emotional response, will provide a gateway to get to the underlying interests of a party.

The less emotionally intelligent and self-aware we are, the harder it is for us to avoid feeling threatened by a stimulus, regulate our emotions and access our cognitive thinking during conflict.

How to use conflict triggers to identify underlying interests

Our responses to conflict triggers are determined by our perceptions and our life experiences. A party's disproportionate emotional response comes from their unique vulnerability or sensitivity. This sensitivity is known as a *hot button*. A conflict trigger cannot be a trigger if there is no hot button response to a stimulus. When we are feeling a response to a trigger, we can unconsciously make a judgment that this other person's values and beliefs may not be compatible with ours.

Exploring the response to conflict triggers facilitates the surfacing of the emotions, concerns, worries or values of parties that may have been impacted. Taking the party back to the event that triggered the conflict, and then asking gentle exploratory questions about their triggered response, will identify the core of what may be affecting them. Exploring the underlying interests of a party moves them from their fixed positional level to connecting with the experience of their original reaction. This is where joint understanding can be created.

Here are examples of questions to explore conflict triggers to reach unconscious underlying interests.

These questions can be asked around the impact on the party, the emotions that surfaced for them, their worries and concerns and their needs.

Subject matter	Mediator's questions
Reflect back what was said	Jean, you mentioned earlier that you felt threatened by the way in which Dan responded to you...
Conflict trigger	When did you first feel threatened, or know that there was tension? What was it that Dan said or did that evoked that reaction in you?
Impact	When you first felt threatened, how did that impact on you? What was impacted that was important to you? What is the one word that would describe it?
Emotions	What thoughts came up for you when that happened? What might have been the emotions behind those thoughts? To what specifically did you find yourself reacting? What did this raise for you? What else did it bring up for you? What was that like for you? About what did you have the strongest reaction/feeling? What is the one word that would describe it?
Worries and concerns	When that happened, what did you become concerned or worried about? What was important to you about this? What was your biggest challenge, worry or concern? What is the one word that you would use to describe this?
Needs	What does this say about your needs? What specifically did you need at that time? When Dan responded to you like that, what needs of yours were not being met? What do you need now?

Method 2: Exploring SCARF® Drivers to Reach Unconscious Underlying Interests

An additional method to discover unconscious underlying interests is to explore with the party any underlying unconscious interests that may have been impacted or threatened, or perceived to be threatened, based on David Rock's SCARF® Drivers of status, certainty, autonomy, relatedness and fairness. This is an effective tool to identify any unconscious needs that may have been threatened.

(Refer to Chapter 3 for a recap on SCARF® Drivers)

Examples of questions using SCARF® Drivers to identify underlying interests:

SCARF® Driver: Status

It is quite common for either or both parties in a conflict to have an underlying need for their status to be respected or restored. An expected, perceived or actual loss of status often results in a feeling of threat or anxiousness, leading to an avoid-threat reflex.

Scenario: Aggressive behavior in the workplace:

- May I take you back to the time this happened; you mentioned that when your boss shouted at you, that you felt undermined. What was it like to feel that you were undermined? What did this raise for you? How did it impact on your sense of yourself and who you are?

- What was this like for you? What were you most worried about? What had you needed most at that time?

After underlying interests have been reached:

- What do you need now so that you no longer feel undermined and your sense of status is intact?

SCARF® Driver: Certainty

The brain is a pattern-recognition machine that constantly tries to predict the future, based on past experiences. If what is happening does not meet a person's expectations, then this can impact on their level of certainty.

Scenario: Expectations versus uncertainty:

- When this happened, what did it bring up for you? What was this like for you?
- What had been your expectations?
- How did those expectations compare with what happened?
- What was the most important thing missing for you? What was this like for you?
- What is it like for you to feel uncertain?
- And what is that like? How is this impacting on you?

After underlying interests have been reached:

- What do you need for the future to ensure that your expectations meet the reality of what might happen?

SCARF® Driver: Autonomy

Issues about a lack of autonomy and self-determination can cause conflict and result in a person feeling out of control, threatened, frustrated or stressed.

Scenario: Business partnership where one partner makes decisions without consulting the other:

- When that happened, what was that like for you?
- What control did you feel you had lost?
- What concerns you most about this? How is this for you? What is it like for you to feel this way?
- What needs of yours are currently not being met?
- What might be the long-term impact if this continues?

After underlying interests have been reached:

- What conversations do you need to have with the other party to ensure that your needs with regard to consultation will be understood and met?

SCARF® Driver: Relatedness

The degree to which we feel a sense of connectedness, similarity and security with those around us can be linked to whether we feel safe or threatened.

Scenario: Relationship breakdown between work colleagues:

- What was it like for each of you when this blew up and you started to pull away from each other?
- What emotions did this raise for each of you?
- What did each of you most need from the other at that time?
- What relationship needs of yours were not being met as the conflict escalated?
- What worried you most about all of this?
- How bad was this worry for you? Rank it from 1 to 10, with 10 being a really serious worry. What influenced you to give it that ranking?
- What do you most miss from the relationship?

After underlying interests have been reached:

- What is needed to get back that trust and to what you miss most in the relationship with each other?

SCARF® Driver: Fairness

The perception of fairness in any situation is not based on cold rational thought processes, but on emotions, which are integral to our judgment of fairness. Neuroscientific research has shown that the amygdala registers a response when we consider that an unfair offer has been made.

Scenario: Commercial negotiation regarding monetary compensation:

- What was it about this that you considered to be unfair?
- What criteria do you use to judge fairness? How would you rank these criteria in order of priority?
- How is what is happening meeting or not meeting your criteria? In what way?
- What is important to you about fairness? If things are not fair, how is this for you? How does this impact you? What is this like for you?
- What is the one word you would use to describe it?
- What is your most important need around this?

After underlying interests have been reached:

- If your need about fairness was satisfied, what could you offer to the other party in return?

Method 3: Exploring Values and Beliefs to Reach Unconscious Underlying Interests

As stated, when parties perceive or experience that their values and beliefs are not compatible with another's, or when they feel these have been infringed or threatened, this will result in them experiencing an avoid-threat reflex.

> We value people, behaviors and events positively if they promote or protect the attainment of the goals we value. We evaluate them negatively if they hinder or threaten attainment of these values goals. Values are critical motivators of behaviors and attitudes.
>
> — S. H. Schwartz [45]

The type of position that a party takes is influenced by their past experiences of conflict, the way they view conflict and the values and beliefs that they have formed. This is the place from where they rationalize their situation and react. However, when parties start to hear the values behind the other's position as a result of questions being asked, they may start to understand that what is beneath the other person's displayed position may not actually pose a threat to them after all.

Definitions of Values and Beliefs

Before giving some examples of questions that can be asked, it is important to cover some theory related to values and beliefs.

Values: A value is a measure of the worth or importance we attach to something. Internalized values reveal themselves in behavior, but professed values may exist only in words. Therefore, to identify the truth of a value, there may be a need to explore behavior and to facilitate the parties to make links between what they say is a value and the actions that they are taking.

Beliefs: A belief is an internal feeling that something is true or correct, even if it may be unproven or irrational.

Note:
Refer to Chapter 14 for further discussion about the role of values and beliefs regarding Cognitive Elements-based questions.

Formation of Our Values and Beliefs

Our values and beliefs are formed by:

- Our experiences during our formation;
- The way our parents or guardians modeled their values and beliefs to us;
- Our culture, education, religion or anything else that influenced us to become who we are.

We may choose to adopt or reject these values and beliefs from our formation, but either way, we will have been influenced by them, even if it was by fighting against them.

Examples of the formation of our values and beliefs:

Values: If a parent has consistently impressed on a child that they must always help others and never say *No* to anyone, that child may decide to accept their parent's values about this, and they may find it difficult to say *No* to a request later in life, even if this request impacts other values.

or

They may reject this value, but either way, they will have been influenced by it.

Beliefs: If a child falls from a horse, they may develop a belief that "Nothing is going to beat me in life and I am going to get up on that horse again!"

or

They may believe that horses are dangerous and decide to never get up on a horse again.

Examples of questions for exploring values and beliefs:

Scenario: Gender transition:

> Joe (Joanne) is eighteen years old. He was raised as a girl but always considered himself male and for the past two to three years has been exploring the possibility of transitioning. He has come out to friends and family and has generally found acceptance, but his mother, Louise, has totally refused to believe that his situation is genuine. She attributes his "confusion" to the fact that his father died when he was twelve, an event which traumatized him greatly, and believes that he is trying to replace this absent male parent.
>
> Louise is very concerned about what the extended family will think if Joe (Joanne) goes ahead with the transition. Louise and her family are very, very religious and have highly principled morals and values, and this screams against everything she believes in. Joe (Joanne) is about to go to college to study architecture, and Louise is threatening to withdraw financial support if he doesn't do as she wishes. Joe has approached his uncle, Louise's brother, for help, and he has advised mediation. Louise has agreed to try it.

Note:
The name "Joanne" is being used with Louise as these questions are being asked in a private meeting.

After talking for a while about the situation she is facing, Louise ends with this statement to the mediator: "Joanne will get over this; the less said the better."

Mediator:

> Louise, you mention that this is a difficult time for you and that you think Joanne will get over it. You also mention that you and your family are very religious and highly principled and that this goes against your values ….

Reflecting on the conflict trigger:
- When Joanne told you about this, what was that like for you?
- To what did you find yourself reacting? What did this invoke in you? What was it like for you when this happened?

Reflecting on the values and beliefs:
- What are your beliefs about transitioning?
- When you talk about values, what do you mean, can you tell me a little more?
- What is it about this particular value that is very important to you?
- You say this undermines everything you consider to be moral, or that you value or believe to be right. What is the most important thing about all this for you?

Hearing the concerns, worries and impact:

- What is challenging you the most? What is it like for you to face this challenge? What is it like for you when your child wishes to do something that you believe is wrong?
- How are you coping with all this worry?
- You talk about losing your reputation within the family; will you tell me a little more about this worry?
- What is the worst thing that could happen?
- You mention you would be devastated if Joanne decided to leave home and not talk to you anymore.
- If this happened, what would be your biggest worry or concern about it?
- You say that you would miss Joanne as you love her very much. You also say you would be worried about how the world would treat her if she goes ahead with these operations because you believe this to be wrong, and others might agree with you and give her a really tough time. And you say that if only Joanne would not go through with this operation, that you would be able to protect her...
- What is it like for you to believe that Joanne could leave home as a result of how you feel about her wishes and that she could have a tough life because of her choice and that you would not be there to protect her?

Other values:

- What are the values you hold about being a parent to your children? And what are your values about a parent/child relationship? How important are these values to you? On a scale of 0 to 10, with 10 being high value, where would you rank it?
- How would you rank the importance of your values to you about what Joanne wishes to do?
- Louise, you say you are now struggling with these two values being mutually exclusive and clashing with each other...
- What might be the outcome if you hold tight to your value about it not being right that Joanne transitions? What might happen if you were to let this value go?
- What might be the outcome if you hold onto your value about parents and parent/child relationships being so important to you?

- What might happen if you were to let this value go?
- What are your overall conclusions at this stage, Louise?

Introducing a possible future narrative:

- What would it be like for you if it was one year from now and you had been able to find a way through this that would have met the values and needs of both you and Joanne?
- What overarching value would you have created that would have helped you to deal with this clash of values — one where you are not struggling with your religious beliefs as well as not worrying that Joanne might leave home and have a very tough life?
- What would you both have needed that would have helped each of you?
- You mention that the shock of all this has been difficult for you, but that if Joanne waited a year before starting the transition, this would help you to get used to the idea and to talk to your family about it without any rush or pressure.
- How would it be for you to have this conversation with Joanne in mediation?

Note:
S4: Cognitive Elements-based questions, discussed in Chapter 14, are helpful when phrasing questions about values and beliefs. Future Focus questions, discussed in the next chapter, will help to focus on future possible narratives.

Difficulties Reaching Agreement with Values-based Conflicts

Values-based conflicts can be the most difficult conflicts to manage. But there are some other methods that may help:

1. Translate values into needs and then ask needs-based questions
2. Create increased understanding between the parties
3. Look for commonalities
4. Discuss the effects of holding or losing this value

1. Translate Values into Needs and Then Ask Needs-based Questions

- What is it that you need from each other that you are not getting?
- What is important to each of you about this need?
- What is it like when you don't have this need satisfied?
- What exactly do you need? How could this need be met?
- If you had this need satisfied, what would it give you? What could you offer to Joe (Joanne)?

2. Create Increased Understanding Between the Parties

At appropriate times during the mediation process, it is important to ask each party to hypothesize about what may have been going on for the other party (S4: Other People questions), because if one party observes from this exercise that the other party understands them, it can help them to shift their thinking and not remain so entrenched. However, caution needs to be exercised about this as the mediator needs to know that the responses from a party to this question, while the other party is in the room, will not fuel the conflict further. Therefore, the questions may need to be asked privately first.

Use S4: Other People questions to increase understanding:

- What might Joanne have observed about you during your struggle with this issue?
- How could you help Joanne to understand what this has been like for you?
- What else might Joanne need you to know to be able to fully understand you?
  - With what might each of you be struggling in trying to understand the other?
  - If you were in Joanne's shoes, with her thoughts and feelings, with what might you be struggling?
  - What might be important for each of you in all this?

Note:

The full range of Other People questions would be very valuable to use in the above situation.

3. Look for Commonalities

If it is not possible to create understanding between parties, then look for commonalities between them and use these as a basis for reaching solutions for at least some parts of the dispute, if not all parts.

Example:

You both say that you did not manage this well; if you were to go back again with the knowledge you have now, what might each of you do differently?

How could this learning be included in an agreement?

4. Discuss the Effects of Holding or Losing This Value:

- What is it about this that is important to you?
- What would happen if this value was threatened?
- What does the holding of this value give you? What does it not give you?
- What is the cost to you of holding onto this value? What would it take for you to let this value go? With what could you replace it? How could this be managed?
- What could change so that you do not feel that your value is under threat? What would that be like for you?

When Values-based Conflicts Are Not Solved

If a values-based conflict is not completely resolved, then accept and acknowledge that this is the case. When understanding has not been reached at underlying interest level, then any agreements made when parties are still at positional level need to be teased out thoroughly. Agreements made without reaching underlying interests need to be comprehensive and detailed to ensure that every eventuality is covered. They need to be vigorously reality tested to guard against any misinterpretations post-mediation.

As the emotions of a party who is still in a "positional" stance may still be high, one of the ways of supporting them to think cognitively is to ask S4: Future Focus questions. These questions change the state of the parties from one of hopelessness and annoyance to one of cautious possibility.

Example of a Future Focus question:

Imagine it is one year from now and the needs of both of you have been addressed, what would have happened that would have caused this outcome? What would each of you have done to have made that happen? What would have changed about your relationship with each other that would have allowed this to happen?

Moving Toward Agreements

Once underlying interests have been reached, refrain from focusing on the past for any longer than is necessary as this may activate the avoid-threat reflex and result in an amygdala hijack. However, it is important to stay in the past long enough to facilitate the parties to vent their feelings and identify their underlying interests. The past can then be used as a platform from which to gather information about the future needs of the parties.

S4: Future Focus questions from the next chapter can be asked at this stage to tease out options for agreement. These questions change the "state" of a party and enable them to shift from their old narrative to a new one. This will facilitate them to activate an approach-reward reflex mode, think cognitively and create solutions.

Key Learning

UNDERLYING INTERESTS QUESTIONS

Underlying Interests questions delve beneath the conflict positions and demands presented by parties in mediation and reach the core of their conflict and the things that are important to them.

Methodology for asking and developing S4: Underlying Interests questions, both conscious and unconscious:

1. Use appropriate body language
2. Signpost and set the tone for asking underlying interests questions
3. Gently reflect back what you are hearing at the start of the process
4. Facilitate the expression of emotions, unobtrusively
5. Identify and use the last words voiced by a party
6. Recognize the difference between positional statements and underlying interest statements
7. Recognize underlying interest feelings within positional statements
8. Support a party who is hesitant to reveal their underlying interests
9. Be aware of the indicators that demonstrate that underlying interests have been reached
10. Work with knowledge of the avoid-threat reflex
11. Ask S4: Future Focus Questions after underlying interests of both parties have been explored

Question tasks for uncovering underlying interests: Both conscious and unconscious

Conscious underlying interests Generic questions	Unconscious underlying interests Additional questions
Conflict positions?	Conflict trigger and the emotional response to it?
Impact?	Impact on SCARF® Drivers?
Emotions?	Values and beliefs?
Concerns/worries?	
Conscious needs?	

Once the underlying interests of both parties have been reached, start asking S4: Future Focus questions.

Hazard Warning

Do not pressure a party to answer a question — proceed carefully and gently, at their pace, and with their permission. Should you inadvertently touch on any past trauma of a party then slowly and gently name the fact that you have touched on it, acknowledge that it must have caused deep pain, and then ask what needs to be in place for the future to address the issues in mediation.

Hazard Warning

It is important to reiterate here that these questions may need to be tested during the initial separate private meeting or in a private meeting during a joint session.

S4: The Shift Thinking Dimension of Questions

To uncover new information and insight, either by exploring and focusing thinking
or by connecting and expanding thinking, leading to a paradigm shift

Journey of Inference Questions
Interpretations, Assumptions, Conclusions, Beliefs, Actions

*Purpose: To identify the link between interpretations and actions.
To explore parties' current narratives and to shift perspectives
toward a new narrative.*

Neuro-linguistic Programming (NLP) Based Questions
Deletions, Distortions, Generalizations

*Purpose: To bring clarity; explore subjective realities,
explore bias and misinterpretations, and create congruency
in communication.*

Distinction and Difference Questions
People, Parts, Contexts, Opposites, Spatial, Comparisons,
Time Span, Measurement or Ranking

*Purpose: To bring clarity, relevance, measurement, boundary
and a different perspective to the conflict.*

Reflective Connecting Questions
Connecting with patterns and cycles of conflict, both
intrapersonal and interpersonal, and in the broader context

*Purpose: To raise awareness of negative patterns and
cycles of conflict, to deconstruct past unhelpful patterns
and to reconstruct new healthy patterns.*

Cognitive Elements-based Questions
Knowledge; Opinion and Thinking; Beliefs, Values and Attitudes;
Behaviour; Sense of Self/Identity; Environment

*Purpose: To explore inner conflicts and inconsistencies between
perception and reality, and between the six cognitive elements.
To seek a paradigm shift that will restore cognitive consonance.*

Other People Questions
Explore an imagined perspective of the other party, a third party,
a cultural norm or hypothetical parties

Purpose: To open perspectives and create insight safely.

Underlying Interests Questions
Conflict Triggers, Impact, Beliefs, Values and Attitudes

*Purpose: To move the conflict positions of the parties to the core
of their conflict, and identify needs and underlying interests.*

Future Focus Questions
Hypothetical, Conditional, Consequential,
BATNA / MLATNA / WATNA

*Purpose: To move parties off the conflict treadmill and facilitate
cognitive thinking, leading to options and solutions.*

Figure: 17.1.
CREDIT: O'SULLIVAN SOLUTIONS

S4: Future Focus Questions

AFTER THE UNDERLYING INTERESTS OF PARTIES have been reached, and when there is no new information to be gained by continuing the conversation, the mediator asks Future Focus questions to move parties out of their cycle of conflict and facilitate their cognitive thinking. This should lead to the identification of appropriate options and solutions. To ask these questions before this has happened might result in one or both parties blocking progress, as they would feel that they had not been heard and understood effectively and that the mediator was forcing them to a solution before they were ready.

If you ask a question that is problem focused, you may get responses about the problem accompanied by negative emotions regarding the past. If you instead ask an effective S4: Future Focus question, then the response will include the opportunities and possibilities for the future with accompanying positive emotions. To do this, ask a party to consider a world in which the problem has been solved. Then use Future Focus questions to generate connections with a possible future perspective that will expand possibilities. These questions paint a possible hypothetical, conditional or consequential picture on which parties can reflect. They change the state of mind of a party and bring them to a place where they can look at their conflict differently, outside their current paradigm.

How Do Future Focus Questions Work?

As covered in Chapter 3, our brains are hardwired to be more sensitive to pain than to reward, and brain research reveals that focusing on problems or negative behavior reinforces those problems and their linked behaviors. Staying in the past any longer than is appropriate may unnecessarily activate the avoid-threat reflex and keep the parties on the treadmill of blame and attack. But when mediators concentrate on asking questions that take the awareness and focus off the negative past and connect instead with future potential solutions, new neural pathways and thinking patterns are developed in the brain. Asking a question by connecting to a future perspective lessens the possibility of the activation of a party's amygdala, resulting in their increased ability to think cognitively. When safety and certainty about the future seem more possible, parties are more open to agreeing a way forward.

> Brain research reveals that focusing on problems or negative behavior just reinforces those problems and behaviors. Therefore, the best coaching strategies focus on the present and future solutions. This requires the development of new neural pathways in the brain and learning new thinking patterns.
>
> — Geoffrey Schwartz, Research Psychiatrist
> at UCLA School of Medicine [46]

Asking Future Focus questions is a way in which to change a party's past negative narratives to a more positive narrative. Once this is achieved, their avoid-threat reflex will reduce and their approach-reward reflex will start to activate. Asking Future Focus questions is a powerful way of creating new paradigms for parties that result in possibilities for action and solution.

When to Ask Future Focus Questions

When parties have vented their emotions, when underlying interests have been identified for both of them, and when there is no further new information or insight to be gained by continuing to discuss the past, then using Future Focus questions will bring parties to a more constructive state.

These questions are used:

✓ When parties are unable to see outside their conflict and move from the merry-go-round of blame and counter-blame to a new narrative, with possibilities for the future

✓ To identify the learning from the past and use it to reach agreement for the future

✓ To facilitate regret by asking parties what they would do differently if they could go back to the conflict with the insight they have now gained

✓ To safely explore and reality test any potential implications and outcomes from possible decisions or agreements

✓ When a party is hesitant to make an offer unless they know the other party will reciprocate

✓ If a party is threatening to leave the mediation process and a mediator needs to ask reality-testing questions

Methodology

The value of Future Focus questions is that they move parties to a positive state where they can think cognitively and imagine a future without the problems that brought them to mediation. As parties see possibilities beginning to emerge during this future-focused conversation, they become more open to negotiating more collaboratively with each other.

While it is important to go to the past to find out about the parties' issues, needs and underlying interests and the impact the conflict has had on them, this information then needs to be used as a box of experiences that can be developed as a platform to get to an imagined safer future.

Example:

- If Tom had handled that differently, how would that have been for you?
- You both mentioned that the past was difficult; what do each of you need to ensure that the future is less stressful?
- What learning could be used from this to create a future that is acceptable to both of you?

If parties are not supported to look toward the future after they have vented their thoughts and emotions, then the conversation between them may go around in circles as they repeatedly use the same negative narrative pattern to describe their position. Initially, parties may slip into their old narrative of blame, so a question that has a future focus needs to be managed well by a mediator and kept positive and focused only on a future narrative.

Example:

Mediator signposting:

I would like to ask each of you some questions, and I know I am being a little directive, but it would be useful if you would keep your responses in the positive. I will give you plenty of time to say anything else that you may need to say afterwards if you consider it necessary.

Mediator asking the lead-in question:

Tom, if this was working well, what would it look like for both of you? I will ask Karen the same question in a moment.

Party:

>Well, she will need to never do that again! And…

Mediator:

>Tom, may I please come in here for a moment. I would like if you would keep your responses positive. If you wish to add any other concerns, I will give you plenty of time to voice them in a moment. Just for now, if this was working well, what would it look like for both of you?

Types of Future Focus Questions: Hypothetical, Conditional and Consequential

Future Focus questions are developed by connecting parties with a future possible perspective that may be hypothetical, conditional or consequential.

1. Future Focus hypothetical questions ask a party to imagine a future that is working well.
2. Future Focus conditional questions ask a party what they would do if certain stated conditions were in place.
3. Future Focus consequential questions ask a party about potential outcomes from the decisions they may make.

Future Focus Question Structure

Future Focus questions usually contain the word *if* and may be prefixed as follows:

>If…
>What if…?
>What could happen if…?
>What might happen if…?

As the parties become more comfortable about the prospect that the conflict will be resolved, then the mediator can make the above question even more powerful by changing the word at the start of the Future Focus question from *If* to *When*.

Examples:

Hypothetical Future Focus question:

>I heard you saying that what happened was a concern for you, and you said that the impact weighed heavily on you. If the future was looking good what might it feel like? What might it look like?

Conditional Future Focus question:

> If everything was to work well for you, and if you were happy with the outcome, what are the things that could have enabled this to happen? What would you have offered to each other about the future?
>
> If you were each to receive what you needed from the other, what might you offer in return?

Consequential Future Focus question:

> What could be the consequences of this decision?
>
> What might be the advantages/disadvantages of this decision?

1. Building Hypothetical Future Focus Questions

To build this series of questions, first ask the parties to envisage a future without the problems of the past, then ask questions that support them to link that future with their learning from the experiences of this conflict. Then facilitate the parties to build a strategy to get to that imagined future, and finally reality test the options with them before they reach agreement.

Examples :

Stage 1: Create a Vision of the Future

Ask parties to reflect on what a future without the problems of the past would look like:

- If this was working well, how could it look?
- If you were supporting each other to work toward a better future, what could you have done?
- What could need to be in place?
- If this was successful, what things could you have agreed with each other?

Stage 2: Link the Past with the Future

Ask parties what they had learned from what had happened in the past that could inform their future agreement:

- If you were to relive that event again with the knowledge that you have now, what might you have done differently?
- What would you have liked the other party to have done differently?
- If that had happened, what would it have been like?

Stage 3: Develop a Strategy for the Future

Ask parties to develop a strategy for how they would ensure that this designed and painted future could become an outcome:

- What worked well in the past that could help you both in the future?
- How could you take this into the future?
- If you were to take small steps toward agreement, what might these steps be?
- If that part was solved, what could that give you? What other areas could you attempt to solve?
- If you were supporting each other to work toward a better future, what could each of you do?
- What are all the options that could be considered to ensure that a positive outcome is achieved?

Stage 4: Reality Test the Options

Ask parties what need to be the criteria for testing the workability of any options for solutions, and then test all the options proposed against the criteria set by the parties:

- Let's look at each of the options and see how they might work.
- What are the advantages/disadvantages of each of the options?
- What might be the challenges and how might you manage them?
- What undertakings do you need to give to each other?
- If it was two months from now and you had both kept to the agreement, and if you had started to build up some trust with each other, where would you be on a scale of 0 to 10 regarding being able to work with each other effectively? With 10 indicating "very well."
- What are all the things you would have done to have made that ranking result possible?

Stage 5: Agree on the Future

- What are all the options that will meet your needs and interests?
- What agreements could be put in place?

2. Building Conditional Future Focus Questions

Future Focus conditional questions are built around what a party might do if certain conditions were in place. Questions that use the conditional tense rather than the present tense will often invite greater reflective speculation, which will help shift the thinking of the parties regarding their future options. This gives the parties an opportunity to see what options might be possible if either of them made a different decision or employed different behavior in the future.

The process of asking conditional questions enables each party to see that the other party could shift their position if certain conditions pertained. It gives parties a safe view of the future before they actually make any commitment.

Examples:

Focusing on the past to move toward the future:

- If you understood each other, what could happen?
- If you both really listened to each other, what would you like to know or understand?
- If you felt that Karen was really listening to you, what might she understand? What would you like her to know or to understand?
- If you were to begin to understand each other's perspective, what could start to happen next?
- Karen, Tom has just said that if he could go back to that event again, he would do things differently. If he had done this in a way that was OK with you, how might you have reacted?
- What might you have done? If Karen had done that, Tom, how might you have responded?
- If you had both changed your responses to each other at that time, how could this have been for both of you?

Focusing on the future:

- If this were to happen again, what could each of you do so that the outcome could be more positive?
- If you were to offer this, Tom, what would you need Karen to offer you?
- If Tom was to offer this to you, is there anything you could offer him in return, Karen?
- If your resolution of this conflict was completely guaranteed, what steps could each of you take right now?

3. Building Consequential Future Focus Questions

Future Focused consequential questions allow the parties to step back from the conflict and explore the potential implications and outcomes from any possible decisions or actions that they are considering.

Examples:

General Future Focus questions and consequences:

- If this happened, what could this mean? What could happen then?
- How could others react to this?
- Would this be a reaction that you would want?
- If you do not wish for this to happen, what action could you take that could give you the response that you would prefer?

Using a Journey of Inference flow for Future Focus consequential questions:

- If you do that, what could happen?
- What meaning could others take from it?
- What could others assume might happen?
- What conclusions or judgments could they come to?
- How could others react to it?
- If this was done to you, what would you take it to mean? What would you assume? What might you conclude? And then what might you do?

Asking Future Focus Consequential Questions to Break an Impasse

If a party is not ready to explore and tease out possible options for solution, then the mediator needs to take it as a sign that the party may not feel that they have been heard sufficiently. There may still be some unexplored or unnamed issues and underlying interests, and it is wise to check this as a first move.

After exploring this with the party, it may be time to ask what are known as BATNA, WATNA and MLATNA questions to facilitate the breaking of this impasse. These questions are usually used as a negotiating technique but can be adapted to mediation also.

- BATNA means the Best Alternative to a Negotiated (Mediated) Agreement
- WATNA means the Worst Alternative to a Negotiated (Mediated) Agreement
- MLATNA means the Most Likely Alternative to a Negotiated (Mediated) Agreement

These questions help a party to become more grounded in reality by facilitating the parties to tease out the potential consequences from any decisions on which parties are reflecting. By thinking through the responses to these questions, mediation parties will understand whether a mediated solution will meet their needs, in comparison to any alternative options.

If a party decides to stay in mediation, this discussion will enable them to clarify their desired outcomes and engage positively in the mediation process from that point onward. Alternatively, asking these questions may lead participants to reach an informed decision about leaving the mediation process. BATNA, WATNA and MLATNA questions are best asked in separate private meetings.

Examples of BATNA, WATNA and MLATNA questions:

The negotiation questions using BATNA, WATNA and MLATNA are consequential questions:

- If you are unable to negotiate a meaningful agreement through mediation, what are all your alternatives?
- What is the best likely alternative to a mediated agreement, if you fail to settle?
- What is the worst likely alternative to a mediated agreement, if you fail to settle?
- What is the most likely alternative to a mediated agreement, if you fail to settle?
- What is your conclusion about the boundaries of your situation?

Setting criteria for a decision-making analysis:

- What are the criteria against which you will assess and measure your decision?
  (Criteria are conditions that any acceptable solution to the problem must meet.)
- How would your BATNA, WATNA or the MLATNA meet these criteria?
- What are the advantages and disadvantages of each of your BATNA, WATNA or MLATNA alternatives?
- What is important to you and what is important to the other party?
- What is important to you and what is not important to the other party?
- What is not important to you, but may be important to the other party?
- What might you lose? What might you gain?
- How does what you may lose compare to what you may gain? What might be the net effect?
- What else could make a difference to your decision?

Using BATNA, WATNA and MLATNA questions with S4: Other People questions

The same flow of questions can be used to ask the party to surmise the hypothetical likely alternatives open to them and open to the other party. This will further focus them on the boundaries around their decision on whether to stay in the mediation process or leave it.

Example:

- If you were looking down at yourself during this discussion, from the position of a balcony, what would you see? What would you advise yourself to do?
- If a third party that you admire was in that balcony looking down at you, what would they see? What might they advise you to do?

These same Future Focus questions can be used to ask a party to surmise the hypothetical likely alternatives open to the other party. This helps focus the minds of a party who may be thinking from an emotional perspective and may not be seeing the realities of the situation.

Note:
BATNA, WATNA and MLATNA questions need to be asked of parties at separate private meetings.

Key Learning

FUTURE FOCUS QUESTIONS

After the underlying interests of parties have been reached, and when there is no new information to be gained by continuing the conversation, Future Focus questions are asked to move parties out of the cycle of conflict and facilitate cognitive thinking, leading to the identification of options and solutions.

Types of Future Focus questions, with examples:

1. Future Focus hypothetical questions ask a party to imagine a future that is working well.

2. Future Focus conditional questions ask a party what they would do if certain stated conditions were in place or certain offers were made by the other party.

3. Future Focused consequential questions allow the parties to step back from the conflict and explore the potential implications and outcomes from any possible decisions or actions.

The same Future Focus questions can be linked with other S4 questions to help shift the thinking of parties.

Future Focus questions are usually prefixed as follows:

> If…
> What if…?
> What could happen if…?
> What might happen if …?

Hazard Warning

It is important to reiterate here that some of these questions may need to be tested during the initial separate private meeting or in a private meeting during a joint session.

Endnotes

1. *The Seven Habits of Highly Effective People*, Stephen Covey. New York: Free Press, 1989.
2. Ibid.
3. *The Structure of Magic I: A Book About Language and Therapy,* Richard Bandler and John Grinder. Palo Alto, CA: Science & Behavior Books, 1975.
4. Selective Attention Test, Daniel Simons and Christopher Chabris, 1999; theinvisiblegorilla.com/gorilla_experiment.html
5. Daniel James Simons is a prominent experimental psychologist, cognitive scientist and professor in the Department of Psychology at the Beckman Institute for Advanced Science and Technology at Illinois University; Christopher Chabris is associate professor of Psychology and co-director of the Neuroscience Program at Union College in Schenectady, New York.
6. The Door Study — Daniel Simons experiment — youtube.com/watch?v=FWSxSQsspiQ
7. Neuro Linguistic Programming (NLP) was created by Richard Bandler and John Grinder in the 1970s.
8. "New Risks in a Flat World: The Growing Importance of Intellectual Property Rights," Jeremy Lack, attorney-at-law, IP consultant and mediator.
9. *The Seven Habits of Highly Effective People,* Stephen Covey. New York: Free Press, 1989.
10. *NLP Workbook: A Practical Guide to Achieving the Results You Want,* Joseph O'Connor. San Francisco: Conari, 2012.
11. Ibid.
12. Robert P. Dilts, NLP University, Modelling with NLP; 1998. nlpu.com
13. Bernard Werber is a French science fiction writer whose work is touched by philosophy and psychology; for this quote, click on "Communications" at bernardwerber.com/frame.php?dossier=unpeuplus/innerview&page=innerview
14. *NLP at Work: The Difference That Makes the Difference in Business,* Sue Knight. London: Nicolas Brealey, 1999.
15. "The Science Behind the Sense: Exploring Cognitive Neuroscience in Decision Making," Robert Benjamin, mediate.com//articles/benjamin46.cfm, 2009.
16. Paul D. MacLean, physician and neuroscientist, Yale Medical School, 1949; Association for Conflict Resolution on May 28, 2010.

17. The terms used in this book are the reptilian brain rather than the hind-brain, the midbrain rather than the limbic system and the frontal brain rather than the neocortex.

18. *Emotional Intelligence: Why It Can Matter More Than IQ,* Daniel Goleman. London: Bloomsbury, 1996.

19. Visual, auditory, kinesthetic, olfactory and gustatory.

20. Emotion regulation is a person's ability to understand and accept their emotional experience, to engage in healthy strategies to manage uncomfortable emotions and to engage in appropriate behavior.

21. "The Neurophysiology of ADR and Process Design: A New Approach to Conflict Prevention and Resolution," Jeremy Lack and Francois Bogacz. *Contemporary Issues in International Arbitration and Mediation: The Fordham Papers*, 2011; Leiden, Netherlands: Martinus Nijhoff Publishers, 2012.

22. David Rock is the author of the business bestseller *Your Brain at Work* (Harper Business, 2009), as well as *Quiet Leadership* (Harper Collins, 2006) and the textbook *Coaching with the Brain in Mind* (Wiley & Sons, 2009). He blogs for the *Harvard Business Review, Fortune Magazine, Psychology Today* and the *Huffington Post,* and is quoted widely in the media about leadership, organizational effectiveness and the brain. Social neuroscience theory developed by Rock explores the biological foundations of the way humans relate to each other and themselves.

23. Published in the *Neuro Leadership Journal,* Issue 1, 2008: med.illinois.edu/depts-programs/academic-affairs/downloads/SCARFNeuroleadershipArticle.pdf

24. *Your Brain at Work,* David Rock. New York: Harper Business, 2009.

25. *Social: Why Our Brains Are Wired to Connect,* Matthew D. Lieberman. New York: Crown, 2013.

26. "The Neurophysiology of ADR and Process Design: A New Approach to Conflict Prevention and Resolution," Lack, Jeremy and Francois Bogacz. *Contemporary Issues in International Arbitration and Mediation: The Fordham Papers,* 2011; Leiden, Netherlands: Martinus Nijhoff Publishers, 2012.

27. *Your Brain at Work,* David Rock. New York: Harper Business, 2009.

28. "The Neural Bases of Social Pain: Evidence for Shared Representations with Physical Pain," Naomi I Eisenberger. *Psychosomatic Medicine,* Vol. 74, Issue 2, Feb–Mar 2012, pp. 126–135; doi: 10.1097/PSY.0b013e3182464dd1. This article was presented at the 2011 American Psychosomatic Society meeting.

29. "The Inherent Reward of Choice," Leotti, Lauren A. and Mauricio R. Delgado. *Psychological Science,* 22.10.2011.

30. "Just Feelings? The Role of Affect in the Formation of Organizational Fairness Judgments," Barsky, A., S.A. Kaplan and D.J. Beal. *Journal of Management,* 37 (1), 248–79, 2011.

31. "The Therapist as a Fear-Free Caregiver," Una McCluskey. *AUCC Journal,* May 2011.

32. "The Neurophysiology of ADR and Process Design: A New Approach to Conflict Prevention and Resolution," Lack, Jeremy and Francois Bogacz. *Contemporary Issues in International Arbitration and Mediation: The Fordham Papers,* 2011; Leiden, Netherlands: Martinus Nijhoff Publishers, 2012.

33. "Putting Feelings into Words: Affect Labelling Disrupts Amygdala Activity in Response to Affective Stimuli," Lieberman, Matthew D., Naomi I. Eisenberger, Molly J. Crockett, Sabrina M. Tom, Jennifer H. Pfeifer and Baldwin M. Way. *Psychological Science,* 2007, Vol. 18; Number 5: pp. 421–28.

34. "Bringing Oxytocin into the Room: Notes on the Neurophysiology of Conflict," Kenneth Cloke, January 2009; see kennethcloke.com/articles.htm

35. *The Black Swan: The Impact of the Highly Improbable,* Nassim Nicholas Taleb. New York: Penguin Books, 2008.

36. *Clean Language: Revealing Metaphors and Opening Minds,* Wendy Sullivan and Judy Rees. New York: Crown, 2008.

37. See cleanlanguage.co.uk

38. "Bringing Oxytocin into the Room: Notes on the Neurophysiology of Conflict," Kenneth Cloke, January 2009; see kennethcloke.com/articles.htm

39. *The Fifth Discipline: The Art and Practice of the Learning Organization,* Peter Senge. New York: Currency Doubleday, 1990.

40. *The Art and Architecture of Powerful Questions,* Eric E. Vogt. Cambridge, MA: Micro Mentor, 1994.

41. Robert Dilts, NLP University, P.O. Box 1112, Ben Lomond, CA 95005, nlpu.com/NewDesign/NLPU-WhatIsNLP.html

42. *1001 Solution-Focused Questions: Handbook for Solution-Focused Interviewing,* Fredrike Bannink. New York: Norton, 2006.

43. *A Theory of Cognitive Dissonance,* Leon Festinger. New York: Row, Peterson & Company, 1957.

44. *Conflict Management Coaching: The Cinergy Model.* Toronto: Cinergy Coaching, 2011.

45. "An Overview of the Schwartz Theory of Basic Values," S.H. Schwartz. *Online Readings in Psychology and Culture,* 2(1), 2012. dx.doi.org/10.9707/2307-0919.1116

46. *The Mind and the Brain: Neuroplasticity and the Power of Mental Force,* Jeffrey Schwartz and Sharon Begley. New York: Regan Books, 2002.

Index

About the Author

GERRY O'SULLIVAN IS A MEDIATOR, trainer, and facilitator with over 30 years of experience in conflict resolution and training. She is an advanced member of the Mediators' Institute of Ireland (MII) and is a member of the US-based Mediators Beyond Borders Consultants Team. She has delivered training internationally with Lawyers Without Borders, in partnership with the Director of Training from CEDR, UK. Gerry delivers accredited Certified Professional Mediation Training in Ireland and has delivered mediation training for the University of Limerick's Master's in Peace and Development program, and she was involved in the development of mediation training in the Law Faculty of Griffith College, Ireland. Gerry is Director of O'Sullivan Solutions, and she lives on the southwest coast of Ireland.

A NOTE ABOUT THE PUBLISHER

New Society Publishers is an activist, solutions-oriented publisher focused on publishing books for a world of change. Our books offer tips, tools, and insights from leading experts in sustainable building, homesteading, climate change, environment, conscientious commerce, renewable energy, and more — positive solutions for troubled times.

We're proud to hold to the highest environmental and social standards of any publisher in North America. This is why some of our books might cost a little more. We think it's worth it!

- We print all our books in North America, never overseas
- All our books are printed on **100% post-consumer recycled paper**, processed chlorine free, with low-VOC vegetable-based inks (since 2002)
- Our corporate structure is an innovative employee shareholder agreement, so we're one-third employee-owned (since 2015)
- We're carbon-neutral (since 2006)
- We're certified as a B Corporation (since 2016)

At New Society Publishers, we care deeply about *what* we publish — but also about *how* we do business.

Download our catalogue at https://newsociety.com/Our-Catalog or for a printed copy please email info@newsocietypub.com or call 1-800-567-6772 ext 111

New Society Publishers
ENVIRONMENTAL BENEFITS STATEMENT

For every 5,000 books printed, New Society saves the following resources:[1]

39	Trees
3,566	Pounds of Solid Waste
3,924	Gallons of Water
5,118	Kilowatt Hours of Electricity
6,483	Pounds of Greenhouse Gases
28	Pounds of HAPs, VOCs, and AOX Combined
10	Cubic Yards of Landfill Space

[1]Environmental benefits are calculated based on research done by the Environmental Defense Fund and other members of the Paper Task Force who study the environmental impacts of the paper industry.